SO YOU'D LIKE TO KNOW MORE ABOUT SOCCER!

A GUIDE FOR PARENTS

by Paul E. Harris Jr.

Illustrations and Cover by:
Jackie Shanahan

Published and Distributed by:
Soccer for Americans
Box 836
Manhattan Beach, California 90266

DEDICATION . . .

To my parents, who taught me what was right.

ACKNOWLEDGEMENTS

Many individuals, both birthright and convinced soccer people, have encouraged me in the task of assembling something new for the soccer parent. I am particularly indebted to those many selfless workers for youth: the coaches, referees, parents, and organizers in the American Youth Soccer Organization and in other youth programs around the country. They are seldom thanked for what they do. Finally, I want to recognize the Federation International de Futbol (FIFA), as they gave me permission to reprint the Laws of the Game, those well-conceived guidelines which govern soccer throughout the world.

Thank you, Doris, for your patience.

INTRODUCTION

This book will not change your lifestyle. Nor is it an attempt to make you give up your sporting or social pleasures, or your natural desire for peace and quiet at home. This short handbook is an effort to create a spark of interest through a bit of knowledge about a game that is capturing many boys and girls in your community and across America.

Your examination of the book will show that you have been spared many points of skill, technique, and strategy. Basically these concerns are those of the coach, a parent like yourself, a person who will be spending at least 50 and maybe 150 hours with your child and his or her teammates. Too often the American parent has been baffled, distressed, and somewhat embarrassed through his own ignorance of the game of soccer. This book will teach you enough about the rules so that you can intelligently watch a game. More important, your two hours of reading may provide you with hints on aiding your child in developing a wholesome set of attitudes toward the game. You may be able to help in working on some skills, as well.

Youngsters who know little of the World Cup (the World Championship of soccer) or of Kyle Rote, Jr., are responding to the joys of soccer, a game which allows for individual differences. Your child is able to play through the efforts of people who have combined an interest in youth and in soccer. Above all, take an interest in what they are doing, by learning about the game and about your child's interest and ability. Both of you will be rewarded!

i

Joan Fosmire is no doubt one of America's foremost soccer parents. As the mother of ten soccer-playing children, she says, "We have been involved in sports for years, but never have enjoyed anything like soccer. Sisters and brothers, all ages and sizes, can play together. Even if a child is not the best on the team he is getting plenty of physical conditioning and having lots of fun. Even I go up to the park and play with the children." The Fosmire family, all 12 of them, are to be found on page 78.

TABLE OF CONTENTS

(Photo by Gabor Lovy)
"When the one Great Scorer comes to write against your name,
He marks not that you won or lost, but how you played the game."

. . . Grantland Rice

1

YOUR CHILD AND SPORTS

You have been given the most important job in the world, that of guiding a child through youth, adolescence, and into early adulthood. Psychologists will tell you that the child's basic personality is determined in the early years through age 7, and that in many ways he is an image of you and what you do.

Your child often learns about his world through the use of his body. When he comes home from school he engages in "free form" play, a self-generated recreation that is really his "work." Through these experiences he learns about individual and group responsibility. In this self-discovery, he will learn of his body's potential, and occasionally its limitations when he tries to do too much. Also, he will learn that playing with other children his own age has its rewards.

Children's play can include adults as well as other youngsters. The strong need for parent-identification carries over to the leisure world of sports and related activities. This need often complements the adult need for physical exercise and a fondly remembered or wished-for youth.

Society, for good or for ill, has created a miniculture of sports enthusiasts. It is the world of youth sports. Many of

1

these enthusiasts work for the image and exposure of a particular sport, some for the betterment of the child, some for both, some for neither. The parent will notice that sometimes emphasis is away from participation where everyone wins, toward competition, where there are few winners. Fortunate is the parent who lives in the community where youth sports organizers strive to make winners of all competitors.

Make no mistake about it, youth sports present no particular magic solution for the problem child. Some learned critics feel that these activities merely accentuate whatever is within a youngster. It is wiser, perhaps, to dwell on what youth sports can do, and have done for participants. Given proper guidance, they can help a child control and order his aggressiveness, and give him a sense of himself and others. They can instill personal discipline and a respect for authority, develop leadership qualities, and a feeling of importance. He will also be able to develop an individual and a team understanding with lesser (and superior) players. Less noble benefits could include regular healthy exercise and a feeling of belonging.

Michael Murphy, founder of the Esalen Institute, feels that sport is a method of reaching for self-realization. He says, in his book, **Golf in the Kingdom:** "Sports as they are practiced are like life as practiced, the transcendent moments are there, they happen, but we lose them like sparks in the wind because our attitude isn't right."

Your child will respond to your attitude. Your placing him in a youth sports program implies a responsibility. At the very least, that responsibility includes knowing the individuals who give of their time for him. Secondly, you should know a little about the sport he is playing. Making an effort to know the game and the coach will help both of you, and may bring you closer together.

(Photo by Bill Bowyer)
Youth often respond to an adult example.

(Photo by Gary Weaver)
Soccer is action and movement, played in a variety of environments.

2

SOCCER,

THE AMERICAN GAME

Soccer, unlike basketball and baseball, had its origin outside of America. The game, probably introduced to the ancient Britons by Roman legions, developed from crude barbarism to the world sport it is today. America's involvement came at the turn of the century, when Scottish, Irish, and English immigrants in New York introduced the game, playing in relative obscurity.

So, the game is not new to Americans, but only now is it gaining widespread interest as a participant and as a spectator sport. Various reasons are offered in explanation for this growth: the coverage of World Cup and Olympic competitions, acceptance of high schools and colleges of soccer, and the growth of the professional leagues. However, one must delve into the game itself for secrets of its popularity among both youth and adults.

SOCCER IS FOR EVERYONE No premium is placed on size in soccer. While it is desirable that certain players have quick reflexes, and others speed or robustness, there is a place in soccer for every physique and level of ability. To use the motto of the American Youth Soccer Organization, "Everyone Plays!" The poorly coordinated, the overweight, the timid, the slow of foot, the slow of mind, and the hesitant youngster can all play alongside the coordinated, the star, the leader. In doing so, the lesser player can still make a contribution to the team and to himself, and feel proud of his achievement.

SOCCER PROVIDES ACTION In soccer everything moves, and nothing is hidden. Players are constantly in motion, and the motion is meaningful. In a one hour game, the ball is in play, moving among and between players for over fifty minutes. Play is open, and easy to follow, unrestricted by complicated plays, team formations, and obscure rules. Spectators are caught up in the kaleidoscopic effect of the action, which changes direction, speed, and pace so often.

SOCCER ALLOWS INDIVIDUALITY Players are seldom restricted by their designated positions, and experience many opportunities to show their skills in the game. Each player will have twenty or more contacts with the ball in every game. Each contact, ranging from a split second to 10 seconds in duration, presents a new challenge, and always in varying circumstances.

SOCCER TEACHES TEAMWORK Just as a ball must usually be controlled before it is passed, a team must work together before it may score. Each player's contribution to the team's success soon becomes evident. Players can create opportunities for teammates merely by moving to open spaces on the field. Each youth interacts with all of his teammates, and is constantly "thinking on his feet."

SOCCER IS INEXPENSIVE, AND IS PLAYED EVERY-WHERE Many of the skills that serve a player can be developed in kicking a tin can. The game is played on grass, dirt, brick dust, hardwood, cement, or sand. While soccer shoes and shinguards are recommended, any athletic shoe without spikes will do. Inventive players and coaches often get by without full fields, or teams, uniforms, or goal posts.

SOCCER ERASES MISTAKES Parents as parents can help reduce the importance of competitions through their own attitudes. Soccer as a game significantly reduces the pressure and anxiety that players experience in some other team sports. Mistakes are quickly forgotten in a game where opportunities come often and when even the best of players mis-kicks, passes inaccurately, and allows goals.

Soccer is no longer a "remote" pastime enjoyed by a few. It is a national sport played by growing numbers of boys and girls, men and women. In the American spirit, its rules and game conditions allow for free, unrestricted movement, open play, and total involvement of its participants. Anyone can afford it, anyone can play it, anywhere, with almost anything! And enjoy it!

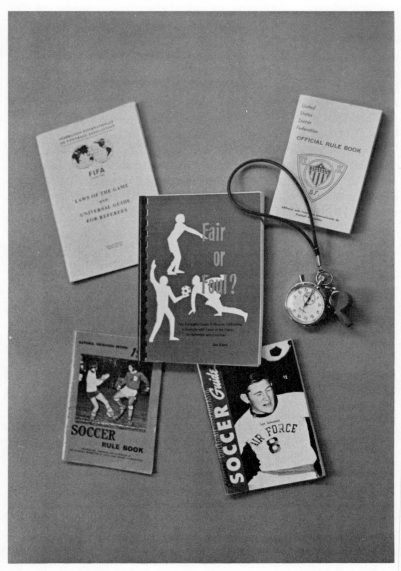

(Photo by Gary Weaver)
Wherever the game is played, soccer rules are the same.

8

3
WHAT'S THAT LITTLE HUMP OUT THERE?

UNDERSTANDING THE GAME THROUGH ITS LAWS

Parents are often confused by what they observe, or think they observe, during a soccer game. To a newcomer, even the markings on the field are a mystery, as are most of the actions of the Referee. ("Can't he see? I saw the ball touch that player's hand.")

The game is best understood by first considering the field, then those who inhabit the field, and finally by what is and what is not allowed.

THE FIELD OF PLAY

Markings: The **center line**, or **halfway line**, divides the field into two halves for kickoffs. It also aids in determining offsides.

The **touch lines**, or **side lines**, form the boundaries for the ball being in and out of play. The ball is put into play from the place where it went out.

The **goal lines**, at each end, also form the boundaries for the ball being in and out of play. When the line is between the posts, it aids the Referee in determining a fair goal. (The ball must be completely over the line, in the air or on the ground.)

9

The **goal area** is for the accurate placement of goal kicks, and the region in which the goalkeeper may be fairly charged.

The **penalty area**, which also includes the goal area, is the area in which the goalkeeper may handle the ball. All kicks awarded to the defense must leave this area before being playable. Direct free kicks in the penalty area against the defense result in penalty kicks from the **penalty spot**.

The **center circle** is the restraining area for all defensive players on any kickoff.

The **corner circle**, or **quarter arc**, is for the placement of balls on corner kicks, when the ball passed over the goal line and was last touched by the defense. When last touched by the offense, a goal kick results.

THE PLAYERS

Each team starts the game with eleven players, one of whom is the goalkeeper, or goalie. (Sometimes called "goaldie" by seven year olds new to the game.) The goalie has different skills, the single privilege of using his hands in the penalty area, and a different shirt. Fullbacks, or backs, are directly in front of him, and are generally durable and aggressive in their defensive role. The linkmen, or halfbacks, create the link between the defense and the offense. They have dual responsibilities of both forming and frustrating attacks. The forwards, or strikers, are usually smaller and often quicker than the linkmen and the backs. They are relied upon for goals, and when the defense is under particular pressure, for taking the ball away from opposing linkmen. Two of the more popular team formations in youth soccer are the "2-3-5" and the "4-2-4".

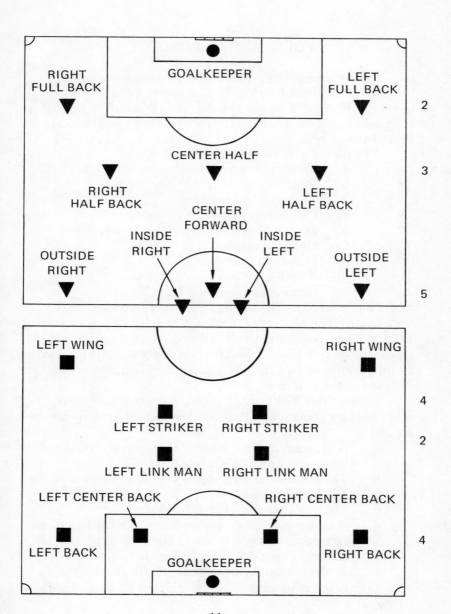

RIGHT
FULL BACK

GOALKEEPER

LEFT
FULL BACK

2

CENTER HALF

3

RIGHT
HALF BACK

CENTER
FORWARD

LEFT
HALF BACK

INSIDE
RIGHT

INSIDE
LEFT

OUTSIDE
RIGHT

OUTSIDE
LEFT

5

LEFT WING

RIGHT WING

4

LEFT STRIKER

RIGHT STRIKER

2

LEFT LINK MAN

RIGHT LINK MAN

LEFT CENTER BACK

RIGHT CENTER BACK

LEFT BACK

GOALKEEPER

RIGHT BACK

4

FOULS AND MISCONDUCT

Players who commit fouls or infractions are penalized by indirect or direct free kicks. The severity of the consequences will depend on the type of foul, its location on the field, and based on what the Referee judges to be the intention of the culprit.

Any player who intentionally:

a. Kicks or attempts to kick an opponent
b. Trips or attempts to trip an opponent
c. Jumps at an opponent
d. Charges an opponent violently
e. Strikes or attempts to strike an opponent
f. Holds an opponent
g. Pushes an opponent
h. Handles the ball
i. Charges an opponent from behind

shall be penalized by the taking of a **direct** free kick by the opposition. The kick, except when a penalty kick is awarded, is always taken from the location of the infraction. Direct kicks may be kicked directly into the goal. Notice that all infractions, except the intentional hand ball, have been directed at the opponent.

Indirect free kicks, when taken, must touch another player before going into a goal, are less serious, and are awarded when:

a. A player plays in a manner that is dangerous to a teammate or an opponent.
b. The goalkeeper takes more than four steps with the ball in his possession.
c. The goalkeeper is charged illegally.
d. A player plays the opponent and not the ball (alert referees say they can watch the eyes of players and thereby judge the intention).
e. A player charges an opponent without the ball being in playing distance. (If it can't be reached

with a leg, it is not within playing distance.)

The Referee signals every indirect free kick by first raising his arm before the kick is taken. His most difficult task is in deciding when a player really intended to do what he did. If there was no intention, regardless of the consequences of the act, he decides, "no foul", and nothing will change his mind. He may also decide that the player or team, even though fouled intentionally, was not placed at a disadvantage through the fouling, so play goes on as if it never happened. Misconduct, however, consists of foul and abusive conduct of all kinds, and is usually dealt with severely.

The continuous play of soccer is one reason for its acceptance among many people. When a ball goes out of bounds, play is restarted by an opponent of the team to last touch it. Throw-ins occur on the touchline, taken over the head with both hands, and with feet on the ground on or behind the line. Goal kicks and corner kicks occur at the ends of the field, and are played without delay from their appropriate areas.

THE OFFSIDE

Chief nemesis of the experienced Referee or player and the beginning soccer parent, this law dominates most of the misunderstanding and controversy in soccer.

Basically, a player should not be in advance of the ball and of at least two opponents when the ball is played in his direction. He is judged offside when the ball was played, not from his position some moments later.

Remember the old grammar books, with all of their exceptions? The offside law is not without its own exceptions, and we must confuse the issue by listing those exceptions, some of which have created arguments since the law was enacted in 1925. (As with the grammar books, the English are responsible.)

A player cannot be called offside if:

13

1. He is in his own half of the field.
2. He receives the ball directly from a throw-in, goal kick, corner kick, or drop ball, or if it was last played by an opponent.
3. He receives the ball from in front of himself.
4. He is not taking advantage of his offside position.

This last one is where controversy arises, as the Referee must judge this player's "taking advantage of the offside position." **Offside positions** may occur anywhere in the attacking half, but there is no **offsides** until the game official decides so.

Read the law in the appendix. It is 78 words long. If you want to watch it in action during a game, you must be located near the touchline, about 20 yards from goal. An average of six offsides are called in games. Watch the foremost attacker. Where was he in relation to defenders when the ball was played? Were you standing exactly even with him, or with the last defender? Really? You're ready — here's your whistle! But, please, don't bother to explain why after you've made your decision. Chances are only you and the player's Mother were watching him when the pass was made!

The laws of soccer have evolved over a period of 150 years, and apply to the game wherever it is played. Minor exceptions occur in the United States where high school and college games are played.

Oh, yes, about that little hump. It's located at the edge of the penalty area, and is called the restraining arc. It is meant to keep players at least ten yards from the ball during the taking of a penalty kick. Some one thought that up 'way back in 1937. That's the most recent change to our sacred field. Don't expect too many more.

EPILOGUE: Some Odds and Ends About the Rules:

1. Occasionally the Referee will stop play for reasons of his own, such as an injury to a player or the presence of the

inevitable dog on the field. Play must be resumed in the most equitable way — a **drop ball** between two players.

2.　In restarting play through a goal kick, corner kick, throw-in, or free kick, a player may not score a goal directly against his own team. Neither team may score directly from a goal kick or throw-in.

3.　The position of the ball is all-important in determining the ball being in and out of play.

4.　Only the Referee's whistle can stop play. It is never required to restart play.

5.　Defensive players must retreat at least ten yards for the taking of any free kick, unless they are standing on their own goal line between the goalposts.

6.　The ball on any free kick must travel its circumference, and may not be played twice in succession by the kicker.

OFFSIDE ILLUSTRATIONS:

1. OFF-SIDE PASS

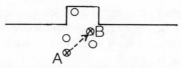

A passes to B who is off-side because there aren't two opponents between him and the goal-line when the ball was passed.

2. MOMENT OF PASS

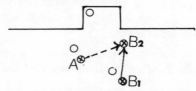

A runs the ball up and passes the ball. B then runs from position 1 to position 2. B is not off-side because at the moment of the pass he had two opponents between him and the goal-line and was also behind the ball.

3. CAN'T GET BACK ON-SIDE

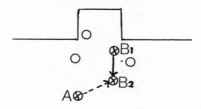

A passes toward B who is in an off-side position. B comes back to get the ball but is whistled off-side because he may not put himself in an on-side position after the ball is played.

4.   DIRECTLY FROM A CORNER-KICK

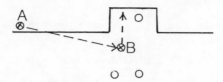

A kicks the corner kick to B who heads it
into the goal. Not off-side because the
ball was received directly from a corner-
kick.

5.   BEING 'IN LINE'

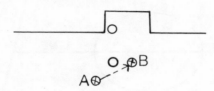

A passes the ball to B who is 'in line' with
his opponent. B is off-side because only
the goalkeeper is between him and the
goal-line.

6.   NOT TAKING ADVANTAGE OF
      OFFSIDE POSITION

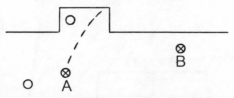

A shoots ball directly in goal. B judged not
offside because he was not taking advantage
of his offside position, and was not interfering with goalkeeper.

17

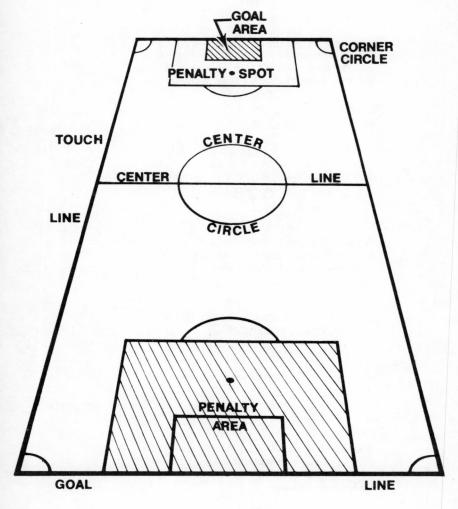

THE INSTEP

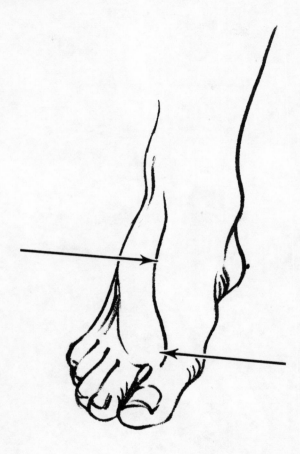

The arched medial portion of the foot is called the **instep.** Any youth player who understands how to kick with the instep will greatly improve his performance in soccer. The drawing above indicates that portion of the foot which is to make contact with the ball. (See page 30, top.)

(Photo by Gary Weaver)
The skills of the game will develop only through practice.

4

KICKING WITH THE TOE?

The skills of soccer are basic and they are individual. The enjoyment you receive from the game will in part depend on your understanding of these skills and how they contribute, collectively, to the team. The pleasure your child receives from soccer is closely related to his skill development through natural agility, coordination, strength, reflexes, speed, timing, and general fitness. More important, however, is attitude.

As you will see in Chapter 10, even the parent who is new to soccer can help in developing a player's skills. The unnatural but important act of heading or trapping the ball, followed by the more natural movements of running, passing, and shooting are often unfamiliar to both parent and child, and deserve your attention.

HEADING

As you have seen in the illustration (opposite), heading can be a frightening experience. Even a wet ball, however, can be headed painlessly and accurately if contact is made at the highest point of the jump, and on the forehead. The whole body enters into the movement against the ball, beginning with the trunk.

"Standing heads", for the purpose of short passing, employ greater use of the arms, and require a bit more room to swing into the ball.

TRAPPING

Ball control is the name of the game, and the ball can be brought under control in only one way, by trapping it without the use of the hands. In each case the player "gives" with the force and direction of the ball, offering that part of the body as a cushion.

In most situations the inside of the foot trap serves the young player. This is the easiest to master.

The leg trap allows the use of any part of the leg, and is a bit more difficult, as the higher the ball is off of the ground, the greater the problem of control.

Chest trapping, allowable with crossed arms over the chest in most girls'competition, will drop the ball directly at the feet, and gives many youngsters confidence in all other traps. Arms are again important for balance, and can almost "cradle" the ball as it is subdued.

Thigh traps, knee traps, sole of the foot traps, outside of the foot traps, and shin traps also provide variety for the player who wants the ball to work for him. Comic relief in a game, but an effective maneuver, was provided on occasion by a famous player who even trapped the ball with his posterior!

VOLLEYING

The volley occurs when a player returns or shoots a ball without first trapping it or getting it under control. It is difficult to perform a volley with accuracy.

The easiest volley is with the inside of the foot, but as with kicking, the instep provides greater power and distance. The player will volley when he does not have time or space to "settle" the ball.

The half-volleyed ball is played on the short hop, immediately after it has touched the ground. The goalkeeper's "punt" is a volley, and his drop-kick is a half-volley.
(Photo by Gary Weaver)

24

TACKLING

When a player is dribbling, or in control or semi-control of the ball, he may be tackled. Tackling is done with the feet, and requires preparation, balance, and follow-through on the part of the tackler. The ball should not be kicked away. It must be **controlled** away from the opponent after the tackle has placed him off balance and at a disadvantage.

There will usually be contact in a tackle. Sometimes it will only be two opposing feet simultaneously meeting the ball. Or, it may include contact of chest, knee, leg, or shoulder.

The sliding tackle, usually employed by defenders, allows the player that extra few inches of reach with the foot. The tackler, after having decided to leave his feet, is at a decided disadvantage, and must have every confidence that he can kick the ball away.

A player has been legally charged, and has been put off-balance.

CHARGING

Charging through the use of the shoulder is allowed. If the ball is being played, there is no possible way that the charge can be violent or dangerous.

THE SKILLS OF
GOALKEEPING

Soccer is an exercise in non-specialization. All players must learn the skills of kicking, heading, tackling, charging, trapping, throwing-in, including the goalkeeper. However, the goalie has an added set of demands placed upon him. They include the use of the hands through punching (the ball, of course), diving, throwing, jumping, catching, deflecting, and the gathering of balls on the ground.

These special skills require all of those skills of teammates, (except heading), plus added agility, sure hands, and a spirit of daring.

Goalkeepers and referees, some soccer people feel, have a special understanding. Goal-mouth action requires special attention from the Referee, for the goalkeeper may be going up, coming down, moving sideways, or just standing still as hard-rushing goal-getters are bearing down on him. If he is injured, play is stopped immediately. And, like the Referee and unlike other players, his mistakes are sometimes known to all.

Throwing-In

Throwing-In can hardly be called a skill, but rather a requirement in the laws, when any ball has passed over the touchline. Logically, the team throwing the ball in is at a disadvantage, for the thrower is out of play, and cannot play the ball without its first touching another player. Note that the ball comes from behind and over the head, and is delivered with equal force by both hands.

Kicking

Kicking, last but not least, brings all parts of the foot into being. The hardest shots on goal and the longest passes always originate from the instep, the hardest part of the foot. Success here depends on the kicking knee being over the ball, the standing foot being anchored, and the toes being pressed down to create a flat instep.

Soccer players **never** should kick with the toe. It is just not accurate, with only the one inch of shoe surface meeting the ball. On occasion you may see a "toe pass" conveniently nudged to a teammate. This is advised only when the ball can be reached in no other way.

The ten inches on the inside of the foot are far more convenient for reliable passing and shooting. Even the beginning player can experience a high degree of accuracy here, and the accomplished player will use the inside of his foot on three of every four passes.

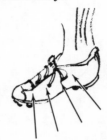

That portion of the inside of the foot normally used — in passing and shooting.

30

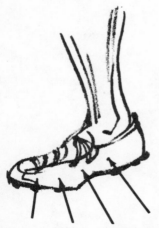

Not to be neglected, but of lesser importance, is the outside of the foot. Proper execution of this maneuver will cause the ball to swerve in flight, even for short distances. The ball is hit slightly off-center, and with an exaggerated follow-through.

The outside of the foot is often forgotten by young players.

As with the toe, the heel is seldom used. "Backheeling", also deceptive, will place a ball behind the player, usually in a pass situation under crowded conditions.

DRIBBLING

Dribbling the ball is merely keeping it under control through a series of "taps" or pushes. More so than with any other skill, the player must have developed a feel for the ball. He may interchangeably use the area to the outside and the inside of the toe. The degree of touch and location of touch will depend on where the player wants the ball to go, and how fast it is to travel. Usually, the dribble is contained directly at the feet of the dribbler.

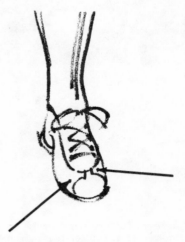

Parts of the foot normally used in dribbling.

(Courtesy of Henry Landauer)
A famous American referee is given the responsibility of officiating a game between two Central American countries. The youth soccer referee has the same tasks as those of Mr. Henry Landauer, the Referee: game control and fairness to all.

5

YOU AND THE REFEREE

"Have no quarrel with the Referee. It is aggravating, I know, to have a goal chalked up against you which ought to have been disallowed, but that is one of the trials which is the test of character. I have played many games in my time, and up till now I have never known a willfully dishonest referee."*

The Referee is referred to with a capital "R" in the Laws of the Game. This is not by accident, as his is an important function, critical to the strict observation of the laws, and probably the most difficult in all of sports officiating. Because he is "in the middle", the Referee is very much a part of the game, and much in evidence. In fact, a ball hitting the Referee results in the same action as when it strikes a player . . . the game goes on.

Whether the Referee you see is your next door neighbor just "doing his part" for the program or a professional official who whistles 100 games a year, his word is law. The Referee is a fallible human, and as such is inclined to err, as are coaches, players, and all other mortals. His errors fall into

*. . .from HOW TO PLAY SOCCER, by J. W. McWeeney. American Sports Publishing Company, 1909, p. 21.

two large categories: (1) Apparent judgement errors and (2) Technical errors. The former group is strictly of a subjective nature, where he may appear to err on any infringement of the rules or on a ball going out of bounds. However, he has made his decision, and he will stick to it, despite the most vehement of protest (although he can always reverse a decision any time before play has restarted). Technical errors, such as awarding a direct free kick where an indirect free kick was to be played, or disallowing a proper substitution, are serious, and can be anticipated by a thorough knowledge of the laws.

Certainly the chief nemesis of the Referee and that of the game itself is the ignorance of the public toward the laws themselves. During a game, the Referee must make at least 200 decisions on stopping play due to fouls or other reasons, and on the awarding of goal kicks, corner kicks, and throw ins. Being the only impartial participant in a highly charged and emotional sport, he knows from the moment he walks on the field that there are those who will be disappointed, even angered and incensed, by some of his decisions.

Unfortunately, much dissent in a soccer game is a direct result of players, coaches, and parents (and sometimes referees) not knowing and understanding the rules. Even if the parent's only motivation in soccer is a "sense of duty" to a child, he should learn a few things about these rules. Chapter three discusses the important laws of soccer, and should be studied with your child. It will help him be a better play-player.

Your child should understand above all that the Referee is to be treated with the highest respect. While on the field, he is the representative of the league, and as such has been authorized to enforce the laws. His mistakes, or apparent ones, must be tolerated in the same way as are the mistakes of players. With some knowledge of the laws and an appreciation of the Referee's task, you and your family will derive more from the game.

EPILOGUE: An Appeal for Referees

With the exception of a "kickabout", no soccer game can take place without the Referee. Each soccer organization therefore needs an average of one referee for each game played each week, and a recruiting and training program is essential to soccer in your community.

Before becoming involved in soccer, each parent must evaluate his own interests, ability, and personality. Although officials, like parents, are blessed with many differences, some generalizations can be made. Due to the job he must perform, the good Referee must be impartial, imperturbable, and not, as David Livingston said, "deterred by the barking of dogs." Generally, the Referee is more of an introvert than is the coach, less inclined to stand up and be heard. He is usually a listener, an observer, and sensitive to the many stimuli that surround him. His trademark is consistency and fairness. All of this is not to deify the Referee, for unfortunately many referees view their job as an excuse for dealing out harsh punishment, and their ego-involvement is full.

The parent who is sensitive in the areas of good sportsmanship and fair play should consider refereeing in his own community. As he gains experience and confidence, he will develop his own Referee Personality. The laws of the game, which are really not complicated, will begin to fall into place. His final achievement will come when he can openly admit to himself and to others that he is very human, and subject to error. Moreover, the lessons to be learned from such experience will aid him in his non-soccer life. He will then know that he has contributed to soccer, and that soccer has reciprocated.

It is a privilege to coach youth. Ms. Penny Lunt, coach of a boys' team
at Eldorado High School in Las Vegas, Nevada, has some friendly words
for the Referee.

6

YOU AND THE COACH

Volumes have been written on coaching and about coaching sports, particularly with the renewed interest in sports and recreation. College and professional coaches sometimes become national figures, quoted and pictured through the media. Little is known, however, about the coach who will spend at least 100 hours with your child as he learns about team sports through soccer.

The coach is usually a parent, like you. If he is not a parent, treasure him even more highly, for he's surely not out there due to family pressure. He may or may not know the rules, the skills of the game or how to get along with youth or parents. He may or may not have a coaching style, philosophy, or aims. We can only say that he is a volunteer, and that he needs your cooperation, and on occasion, your help.

You can best aid the coach by making yourself known to him, (or her) and thanking him for his interest in coaching your child. Then, step aside, let him do his thing, and support him in a minimal way by encouraging your progeny to be punctual and conscientious about attending practices. Go to the games, be enthusiastic, and accept without complaint those small tasks that may be asked of you by team organizers.

If you are attentive, you will learn more about your child, and about the coach, by watching games than you will learn by second hand reports over the dinner table. The classroom of soccer is the open field, and the attitude of the player toward soccer is in direct relationship to the attitude of the coach.

A veteran youth soccer coach recently quipped, "Teaching seven year old youths to play soccer is like driving a car with a very loose rubber steering wheel." The unexpected does indeed come in soccer, just as frequently as in other areas of life, and your coach will learn to live with the unpredictability of youth. That is his challenge, like your own as a parent.

EPILOGUE — An Appeal for Coaches

In the best sense of the word, a coach is an educator, and his sphere of influence goes far beyond the rules and skills of the game. The coach, not the existence of uniforms, league standings, playoffs, trophies, or referees, is the chief difference between the free-form play of a sandlot game and organized sport for youth.

The good coach promotes physical and mental wellbeing, a respect for rules and authority, and a spirit of cooperation. He may well be the most influential individual in your youngster's life. If he exerts personal emotional control, players will do likewise. If he is enthusiastic, the enthusiasm will spread. If he is fair to all and appreciates the effort of each one, players will be supportive of one another.

Parents are a lot like people. They are reluctant to step forward and reveal their ignorances. Although soccer is not new as a sport, it is new as a popular national sport, and much of the new interest has been the result of "first generation" soccer parents. Many of these people never played or viewed the game until they "took over" a team. Most found that learning the skills along with the team, or from experienced players, helped to build an understanding between players and coach.

Part of the beauty of soccer is its simplicity of form, technique, and strategy. The growing number of children who find pleasure in the pursuit of the soccer ball want to share this enthusiasm with you! The recognition that youth are a pleasure and a challenge and that soccer is a wholesome game to be experienced is reason enough to give of your most precious asset — your time as a youth soccer coach.

(Photo by Gary Weaver)
Good sportsmanship also implies being a good winner. A winner is con-
gratulated by Hans Stierle, President of the American Youth Soccer
Organization.

40

7

GOOD SPORTSMANSHIP ...
THE KEY TO ANY GAME

A boys' high school soccer team was seen regrouping for a team cheer in the middle of the field immediately following a crucial goal against its own side. This impressive display of "togetherness" and team spirit, in a moment of near-defeat, was obviously the result of training and discipline, and is one hallmark of soccer as it should be played.

Similarly, the out-of-bounds ball that is chased down, the concern over an opponent's injury, the recognition of well-earned opponent's goals, and the friendly congratulatory words to winners and to the Referee after the game should all be a part of soccer.

It has been stated by concerned soccer officials that the Referee's chief function is to aid players in the control of the game. Even in youth soccer, it is possible for the team captain to be the player most representative of good sportsmanship on the team, and his position is one of honor. He can know something about the rules, and what they mean. He can therefore encourage teammates in their team efforts and discourage them in their protests of referee calls.

Parents can aid by seeing that all players' efforts are praised, and not just the results of their efforts. Players can be reminded that according to the research of the game, shots on goal result in goals only 10% of the time, and that for youth, only 20% of all passes are accurate! If for no other reason, the player who misses a goal should be encouraged to try again, for even a great player misses nine times in ten.

It has been suggested elsewhere in this book that family soccer is a highly recommended sports activity. A parents' game could "happen" just prior to a regular youth contest. Good sportsmanship from parents is worth more than a thousand words of advice to the "hard loser" in the family. His own game could thus be brought into perspective.

If the soccer experience is to be meaningful at all, it should be emotionally satisfying for your child. Soccer affords a full opportunity for expression, and defeat is often accompanied by a good cry. This outburst should not be discouraged, as it has no connection with sportsmanship. Rather, it is a natural release by the child to whom everything is momentarily of importance. The parent can sympathize with, but not minimize, the sting of defeat.

(Photo by Dick Smisek)
"Character is what you are when no one is looking."
... Benjamin Franklin

(Photo Courtesy of John David Heckel, Tulsa (Oklahoma) World.)
Parents participate in a variety of ways.

8

HOW TO PARTICIPATE
IN YOUR CHILD'S GAME

There is a wealth of soccer activity now available in many communities, ranging from youth programs on up through visiting international teams. The chances are that you and your child are learning about soccer together, and that you should therefore attend some games together. Attend games at both your child's level and above. Thus, he will see others of his own age in play, and the two of you can share observations on how "the others" do it. Superior play of semi-professional or professional caliber is exciting and entertaining, even though your offspring may be average, and could not hope to duplicate such skills.

If you are close enough to the field of play as you view the game, you will be surprised by the size of the players. Unlike many other American sports, soccer success comes from skill alone, not skill combined with size. The use of these skills without the use of the hands is an added challenge. Finally, you will observe that soccer is truly the democratic American sport; players are guided by individual initiative, and allowed the freedom to create and to move in patterns that are not set. They are seen operating at various levels of offense and defense, with the ebb and flow of the game constant.

There's no point in distorting the truth. As a parent, you are most interested in your boy or girl, and in how he or she performs in a game. As a disinterested observer, you have seen a few soccer games at other levels, and now you want to learn something more about watching your child in action!

Not every child wants to admit it, but it is a great thrill to play before appreciative parents. Win or lose, your support means a lot. Once you have established yourself as a faithful **team** supporter, your child will benefit greatly. You will begin to know the various players, with their strengths, weaknesses, and problems. Your child will sense your support and encouragement of the weaker players (maybe **he** is one of them), and he will react to your support. In fact, through this kind of support, you could be moulding him into a team leader! If your child is a weak player, he needs that much more support. Your presence and positive attitude will place him in better standing with the team, and the coach will be more tolerant of his weaknesses.

Don't make the mistrake of the soccer Mother who soon tired of watching her son's games because "nothing ever happened at his goal." He may have played an excellent goal, but she tired of watching him do nothing while the game proceeded around him. When you go to a game, watch and cheer for the whole team, not only for your progeny. If you learn the names of the other players, and root for them, too, your child may soon be the most popular player on the field! His peers will pass to him, and the other parents will soon know and cheer for your child as well.

If you have not already discovered it, a soccer game is a happening. Only the most passive parent will not become emotionally involved. When you do, try to confine your remarks to the positive, including occasional applause for the opponent's good play. This does more for your child than all the ready-made speeches on fair play and good sportsmanship.

When you watch a game, watch it closely, for then you can help your child. He will have more than 20 contacts with

46

the ball, some prolonged, in an average game, when he can show his skills. The fluid nature of the game will enable him to do many things without the ball, creating opportunities for himself and for others. Study his movements while he runs "off" (without) the ball, as well as his gestures which tend to support, or sometimes degrade or devalue the efforts of a teammate. Your observations on these points will be helpful to him, for you can be sure that no one else is watching him when the ball is elsewhere. As has been suggested in chapter six, leave all coaching comments on the field to the coach. In most cases, he is the better judge of how your boy is performing with respect to the rest of the team.

You have now become an active participant in your son or daughter's soccer life. And, it is hoped that you will be gathering some order from that seeming disorganization of passes, tackles, shots, saves, and goals that is called soccer.

(Photo by Gary Weaver)
The selection of a ball, much like the selection of a pumpkin, is a very
personal thing.

9

EQUIPMENT

Some years ago a popular promotional brochure illustrated the simplicity of soccer by portraying a group of boys kicking a ball of rags around an empty lot. While this may be the extreme, it is generally understood that equipment requirements are minimal in the game. Buying decisions must be made by the parent, even though required equipment is seldom a necessity in organized youth soccer. With the passing of steel-toed shoes with nail-in leather cleats and the demise of the laced ball, modern soccer equipment brings a variety of attractive choices.

The equipment you consider should be designed for youth and within your means. In most cases, the most expensive equipment should not be considered. Youth are no less hard on soccer shoes than they are on street shoes. Attractive items invite loss through theft, always a problem when groups of youth congregate.

THE BALL

The budding soccer player will want to be practicing with a ball. He should be told that any ball, even a tennis ball, will do for purposes of skill development and coordination. However, he will someday want a real soccer ball, and this important purchase may determine in part the pleasure he receives from playing, plus that of peer recognition. The weight, material, size, color, and coating of the ball should be considered more carefully than the manufacturer's label.

Weight. The weight of the ball should be equivalent in ounces to the child's age. An eight year old should use an eight ounce ball. Since the ball will last two or three years with proper care, let him "grow into" the ball. Girls prefer slightly lighter balls.

Material. If your child dribbles through the streets, shoots against walls, and supplies the ball for neighborhood kickabouts, a durable rubber playground ball is suggested. However, if grass and dirt fields are the accustomed surface, the ball should be made of leather and stitched, as opposed to other materials and non-stitched. The feel of the ball is very important. Compare the ball you want with a top-quality handstitched leather professional ball. Bounce it, listen to the sound, compress it, feel the suppleness. Look at it, and see the roundness.

Size. The player deserves the satisfaction of seeing his kicked ball travel a reasonable distance, without being too heavy to lift or so light that it will "sail." A smaller sized ball develops skills, but should never for game purposes be less than 23 inches in circumference. Manufacturers cannot make large light balls out of good quality leather. Therefore, a good quality leather ball (of proper weight) for a specific age should be as large as possible within the desired weight for that age. All balls should be slightly deflated when not in use, particularly after play on a wet field.

Color. The 32 panel black and white soccer ball, first introduced in the mid-1950's, is highly recommended. Spin can be visually determined, almost a requirement in practice and in games. All-white balls are sometimes successfully used for night practice and games.

Coating. Effective coatings which last the life of the ball are available only with very expensive balls. Ripple coatings, hard spray coatings, and laminated balls all are semifutile attempts to deal with the problem of moisture. Soccer purists hand-rub leather balls with a protective coating. Allpurpose rubber coated balls are recommended for wet weather, since there is no reasonably-priced water resistant ball made from leather. For dry field play, bring out the leather balls.

Shoes. Young players will outgrow their shoes within a year, if they do not first fall victim to mud, water, and the general ravages of wear. Unless the child is the first of twelve soccer players in the family, high priced shoes are not recommended. Shoes must have:

1. Lightness in weight.

2. Soft rubber-molded cleats. The more cleats the better, for they will reduce injury and serve as a cushion for the foot. Removable cleats wear down, must be replaced, are slippery on hard surfaces, are dangerous to self and to opponents, and cause knee injuries by not allowing rotation of the foot and leg.

3. A correct fit. Reasonably loose fits will allow for an extra pair of socks, if this is desired.

Soccer Clothing. Since uniforms are worn only on game days, other soccer clothing must be considered for practice. Usually the option of the coach, this uniform may vary with climate and field conditions.

A carefully chosen sweat suit will last three years, for the player will grow into it. If one prolonged cold is prevented, it will pay for itself. It may be used for practice, travel to game sites, and for leisure non-soccer wear. Colors should be bright for visibility in practice and for the safety of early evening travel from field to home.

Light, durable shin guards last until they are lost, and should be required with long socks at all practices and games. Youth players often claim to be encumbered by shinguards, and note the habits of older players (usually professionals) who shun the standard shinguard. Some professionals, it must be noted, are more skillful at avoiding injury, and exhibit more control in tackling and in ball handling. These players are nevertheless exposing themselves to needless injury.

The time and effort in basic equipment selection is well-spent. Much depends on one's finances, the size of the selection, climate conditions, and the personal requirements of age and sex.

(Photo by Bill Bowyer)
Standard post-game equipment for girls . . . win or lose.

Parents and youth can both
be inventive in finding
ways to improve
performance.

"I like playing soccer because
it's a sport where you're always
moving and you can play for
five or six months without
getting tired of it. It builds up
your body, physically and
mentally. You don't have to
win to have fun. Remember,
it's for boys and girls alike."
Arno Portegies, age 14

54

10

GAMES CHILDREN PLAY

In what is probably the most impressive sports instructional film ever made, the international star Pele of Brazil, in THE MASTER AND HIS METHOD, demonstrates the agony and the repetition which is necessary in improving one's soccer skills. Totally inspirational, the four part document shows the dedication that is required for greatness. Equally important to this observer was the presence of Pele's teammates developing their talents, lesser though they were. Without the skills of teammates, Pele's own would be worthless.

Your child's coach has at least fourteen other players who need his attention, and there is not enough time in any practice for total skill development. Any time your child spends with the ball will make him a better player, and you can encourage him through suggestion or through actual participation. Every player can be shown that skill games, like soccer games, can be fun.

Using Games to Overcome Fear:

1. "That 28 inch spheroid wasn't meant for my head", both you and your child may think. Hold the ball and have the player try to head it out of your hands. Or, sit down and

head it back and forth. Both of these exercises will generate confidence and develop full use of the trunk and neck.

2. Hang a tether ball from a tree, about four inches higher than the player. He can jump and head, with no real impact to the head from the experience.´ Vary the height for increased jumping. Lower it close to the ground for kicking exercises.

3. Have the player roll the ball toward you, following three feet behind the roll. When it reaches you, kick it at him gently, then a bit harder each time. He will learn not to turn his back on a tackle or on a kick. So will she.

Using Games to Develop Kicking Skills

1. No one uses the toe when playing barefooted. Soft grass in the park or beach sand provides the perfect kicking surface for barefoot kicking, and don't forget to deflate the ball slightly. A feeling of "oneness" with the ball will result. If the ball stings, put on a sock.

2. Aim at a series of targets that can be knocked down from short then from longer distances. First do with the inside of the foot, then the outside, then the instep. Now try the left foot.

3. Back to the tether ball. It can be held, at arm's length, from a three foot rope, for developing the instep, the outside, and the inside of the foot. As in rope-skipping, this develops coordination.

4. Anchor the tether ball to the ground. Try some kicks with the inside, then the outside of the foot. No time lost in retrieving the ball. Now try the weak foot. Someday the young player must learn that the left foot can be used for more than a support.

Using Games to Develop a Sense of the Team

1. Leave the soccer ball at home, and play basketball. Show how players must leave crowded spaces to create openings for receiving passes. The principle is no different in

soccer. Try floor hockey, or speedball.

2. The "heads up" drill. Passes are always made with the head up, shots always taken with the head down. Player must look up immediately after he has the ball under control, so he may find his teammates. Move away from your original position after you pass to him. Does he know where you are?

3. Have players pass the ball around with their hands, as in team handball. The final maneuver must be a heading of the ball into the goal or past a barrier. This teaches teamwork, develops heading skills, and instructs in the importance of calling for the ball when it is needed.

Games for Ball Familiarity

1. Juggling the ball with the feet is not for show-offs. This activity aids in coordination and control, though seldom used in games. This may be a bit discouraging at first, for it looks easy. First try it in the living room with a balloon.

2. Pass the ball quickly back and forth between the two of you, with no stopping it. This will teach the player to quickly get rid of the ball. Variations could include the alternating foot, only the left foot, the outside of the foot, or inside of the foot.

3. The shifting of the ball back and forth from one foot to the other develops coordination and confidence. End each of these exercises with a pass or a simulated shot on goal.

4. "Four square", akin to "hop skotch", is played with two or more players. The object is to kick the ball across the center line to a square that is called out by the kicker. The ball, which should be of playground variety, should be played after only one bounce.

A Game for Understanding and for Variety

Soccer's answer to Monopoly is a game called Subbuteo. A table-top game with the full complement of players and all of the accoutrements of soccer, it is excellent for showing team formation and play. An excellent gift for the player

who has an occasional rainy afternoon. Developed by Subbuteo
Sports Games, Langton Green, Turnbridge Wells, Kent, England.

The above games are mentioned to only show the variety
of options that are open to the parent who knows little about
the sport, but who wants to learn a little. There is no limit to
the number of games that may be played in preparation for
soccer understanding and participation, on any surface and in
the smallest of areas. Only two requirements must prevail if
the game is to be at all meaningful. First, at least one game
skill or body-building exercise must be employed. Secondly,
the player must have some feeling of success in what he is
doing. Perhaps his success will come by being with you and in
discovering his talents with and through you.

(Photo by Gary Weaver)
Young players readily respond to new play environments.

(Photo by Gary Weaver)
Using halftime to the best advantage.

11

ORANGES AT HALFTIME?

For many parents, their total participation with the local youth soccer program involves providing players with oranges at halftime. On occasion they may come to a game, but only if pressed to do so, and only under the best of climate and game conditions.

Unfortunately, the reluctant soccer parent is often regarded as a "lost cause" in the soccer environment. Dedicated organizers (soccer nuts) shake their heads and usually agree that most of the work done in any organization is performed by a very small percentage of the adults. This need not be so in youth soccer, for there are ways to involve everyone.

People respond to a direct, positive approach. A general appeal in a newsletter will never elicit a response. Direct, personal contacts with "low-profile" parents will generate better results. Attempts to bring parents and players together in work pursuits is also advisable.

The coach who meets his soccer parents informally and in a social atmosphere is wise, for he will learn more about his players through the parents than he will in countless field sessions. He will then gain the support of parents when it comes to the needed extra practices, typing, telephoning, and time away from planned family activities.

There is no parent, anywhere, who has nothing to contribute to the youth soccer program in the community. His child is benefitting from your and from other people's efforts. So, show the parent that working for the sport is working for the child. The strength of any organization is no greater than the sum of its active participants, and soccer deserves full participation.

(Photo by Dick Smisek)
Waiting for the Orange.

(Photo by John Fever)
The coach and the referee are usually best qualified to decide if an injury is real.

12

INJURIES AND OTHER
PAINFUL EXPERIENCES

Youth who play soccer are no different from other youth. They are growing, and with this growth comes needs. The unusual physical and emotional needs of the youth soccer player should be discussed between parent and coach. The condition of a young player with asthma or a trick knee should be openly brought to the attention of the coach. Less obvious human frailties, such as a tendency to exaggerate pain, are equally important to the coach who wants to do the best for his players.

Soccer will develop and improve total body coordination for your child, through running, heading, throwing, kicking, trapping, and walking movements in practice and on the field. With the skills of the game will come the development of a set of physical qualities: speed, reflexes, endurance, and heartiness. A simple series of exercises before each practice or game session will aid your child in avoiding injuries. Simulations of moves in the game are most appropriate, with special emphasis on muscular warmup.

To some players, being hurt can be a good thing. Injured players often draw attention, much more than the uninjured, healthy team member. Since there is almost no injury in soccer that is not made better by the application of ice, a handy ice-

pak is perhaps the best way to anticipate the occasional bruise
or scrape in need of attention. Players feel important, and with
youth this kind of cathartic "stroking" is advised. "Compress,
ice, elevate, and play" can be the slogan for the injuries which
require some attention. Less serious ones the players must live
with, accompanied by encouragement from the sideline.

On an injury where there is the slightest *danger* to your
child, he should be immediately removed from the game. The
younger the child, the more conservative the coach should be
in his decision on "leaving him in." Medical authorities claim
that if, when you arrive at the scene of an injury, the player is
in the same condition as when it happened (10-15 seconds
previous), take him out. And, any player who loses conscious-
ness, even for a short time, should be removed for the game and
possibly for the season.

Physical educators have classified soccer as a non-contact
competitive sport. While this label may be questioned, it is
undeniable that soccer is a safe activity. There is no unusual
stress on any one part of the body. The entrance of molded
rubber cleats and lightweight shinguards into the game coupled
with the exit of steel-toes shoes have combined to eliminate
traumatic injuries from equipment. The ball is seldom kicked
with force which would do damage to the recipient of the kick.
"Youth soccer, even among large programs, to date has had
so few injuries that no data is available to be analyzed," according to J.D. Garrick, M.D., Head of Sports Medicine at the
University of Washington.

The parent should remember that most bruises in youth
soccer are those to the psyche of players, and these, like
bruises in the home, can be salved by patience and understanding.
While the game of soccer is an emotional one, it does not have
to be pressure-packed, a condition leading to emotional
injuries. Injuries resulting from the ball, players' equipment,
the field, and twenty-one other bodies on the field are usually
meaningless. The bumps, scrapes, and bruises are no different
from those brought home from a weekend in the mountains.

(Photo by Dick Smisek)
Sometimes the goal can be a very secure place.

(Photo by Bill Bowyer)
Vive la difference! Girls have taken to soccer everywhere.

13

SOCCER FOR GIRLS

The 1964 Tokyo Olympics and its women's volleyball brought new world attention to women's team sports. Introduced for the first time, it proved that team competition was no longer the province of men, and that the public would respond favorably to women's team athletics.

The early success of girls' soccer programs in the United States has nothing to do with women's liberation, and little to do with volleyball in Japan. Rather, it is the result of advanced thinking by sportsminded people who recognize that soccer is a healthy and socially acceptable outlet for aggressive and competitive needs, in addition to being plain fun.

Co-educational, mixed soccer has proved successful in certain areas where not enough players yet exist for full, segregated programs. Although mixed soccer is not recommended beyond age 12, girls are often bigger and more mature in the 7-11 age group, with aggressiveness not being a problem in play. Therefore, they fit in well with the boys' competition and add a new dimension to the games.

As with the boys, soccer provides an activity for girls whose abilities are limited, as well as for those who are athletically inclined. In soccer, a weak, passive player is not as obvious as she would be in girls' basketball or volleyball. She will soon discover the logic and reward of running off (without) the ball and of sharing it with teammates. Soccer appeals to girls because it is above all a very social sport, with action and movement that growing youngsters need. Girls have been found to develop skills as quickly as boys, given a modicum of coaching.

Rules for girls' soccer do not differ, except that a somewhat lighter and slightly deflated ball is recommended. According to FIFA, the world body of soccer, "A hand ball does not apply to a woman player if she engages in fending off of the ball for the purpose of avoiding injury, as long as the action is both necessary and protective." This applies only to the chest. However, as referees and coaches debate the point, the girls go on playing, and as of this writing there is no record of a girl's chest injury in soccer.

Although post-game tears *do* flow, coaches in girls' soccer seem less intent on winning, are more inclined to shift players from one position to another, and coaches tend to build up an excellent personal rapport with the girls. Boys are often allowed and invited to practices, both for team morale and for demonstrating skills. Some coaches even scrimmage their girls against younger boys, in order to develop a more aggressive attitude with their team.

Parents who take an interest in their girls' soccer activity will find the door wide open for participation. Active parent involvement could include helping at early-season sessions, where attrition rate may be high, and when the coach is just beginning to know his team. Since girls develop a closer sense of comraderie, some parents can contribute by planning post-game activities unrelated to soccer. Others should know that girls like the feminine frills of sport, such as attractive uniforms, unusual warmup or game caps, team ribbons for the hair, or a team banner. Parents should know that girls relate very well to men in sport, and should be on the lookout for mature high school players who have the ability and authority which coaching requires.

As girls enter the first and second years of high school, interest remains, even among average players. Unfortunately, regular girls' programs do not widely exist at the high school level. Parents are encouraged to involve themselves in school athletic activities, and to awaken school authorities to the wholesome benefits of the game.

(Photo by Gary Weaver)
High school soccer, particularly at night, is an exciting spectacle.

14

HIGH SCHOOL SOCCER

Soccer in high schools was formerly the province of preparatory schools in the East and of an occasional large-city school. The 1970's however, are bringing a new interest in school soccer competition, and over 3,000 high schools in most states now participate in various league activities. In some cases, the season takes place in the Fall (East and Midwest) and in others the Winter and Spring (Southwest and West). The pressure of colleges from above, with their offering of full soccer programs, and that of youth soccer from below, with their large registrations, will continue to effect a growth in high school play.

Due to the effect of television and students' generally being turned off by organized sports activity, team sports appear to be on the decline in the United States. However, soccer is on the increase at all levels, through college and the professional ranks. This is due largely to the nature of the game — a game where success comes from skill. A full program of soccer, including intramural non-interscholastic competition for the lesser skilled players, as well as freshman, junior varsity and varsity competition for the skilled, is possible at your school. Parents should feel confident in approaching their schools with soccer as a new alternative in their athletic program, with the knowledge that soccer will provide not just *another* outlet for the year-round athlete, but will be reaching a new element in the school population as well.

Once the program has begun in your school, the community must be made aware of it. You must recognize that soccer will probably initially be looked upon as a minor sport, for it will not contribute significantly to the athletic income at the school. An occasional night game, with proper publicity, however, will bring out more people in the soccer community, and this activity is encouraged. An extension of this idea is the cooperative soccer night with local youth soccer organizations, where several games are played under the lights. Where lights do not exist, Saturday morning or afternoon games will serve to introduce the game to the local populace.

Again, it must be remembered that schools respond to community needs, and the interested soccer parent can greatly help to initiate soccer in a school district, particularly in an area where youth soccer, favorable weather, and a modicum of enthusiasm and knowledge of the game is present.*

*For additional information on establishing a high school soccer program, contact The Soccer Advisory Council, 21610 Anza Avenue, Torrance, California 90503

(Photo by Thomas E. Simondi)
One player in pursuit of a ball, one in pursuit of an opponent.

(Photo by Oto Maxmilian. Courtesy of the Los Angeles Aztecs)
Professional soccer provides a new dimension of activity for the young
player. Twenty three cities in the United States and Canada now field
teams in the North American Soccer League and in the American Soccer
League. Tony Douglas of the Los Angeles Aztecs attempts a shot on
goal against Vancouver.

76

15

BEYOND HIGH SCHOOL

Competitive sports such as swimming will retire a participant at an early age. Others, like tennis and golf, know no age limit for achievement. Soccer may be placed alongside volleyball, basketball, and softball as requiring some physical preparation, yet providing recreation and enjoyment far beyond adolescence.

As soccer continues its growth, colleges are providing more opportunities for intramural and intercollegiate competition. Variations on the game, such as sand soccer, indoor soccer, or six-a-side soccer will bring new participants. Women's leagues and family get-togethers for soccer provide a contrast for many who enjoy the recreational aspects of the game.

Quality soccer through semi-professional or professional leagues appeals to youths who should see the game in a variety of settings. Their involvement is even more valuable if skills and tactics are viewed in the setting of highly motivated participants. And, because soccer is on the upswing and its devotees anxious to spread the word, professionals are available to youngsters and parents. Many professional soccer clubs conduct clinics and sessions where player meets player.

Opportunities for soccer play are legion. With our current rage for participation in sport, soccer provides at every turn a chance for all to play, and to reach the heights of one's ability and interest.

Here is America's most active soccer family, the Ed Fosmires of La Mirada, California. Seated: (left to right) Janice (12), Mary (10) and Greg (7); Kneeling: Kathryn (15), Mrs. Fosmire, Ed Fosmire; Standing: Mike (15), Dan (12), John (19), Tom (17), Jim (16), Carol (14). Mr. and Mrs. Fosmire enjoy playing soccer, too.

16

PARENTS CAN PLAY, TOO

Anyone who has seen a group involved in a "kickabout" will agree that above everything else it enhances health and fitness. The constant movement on the field, the continual use of legs, body, head, and feet is an exhilirating activity, both safe and inexpensive. Moreover, soccer is a social sport, an excellent means of bringing people together and involving them all. The communication and verbal exchange is part of the game, with no one being neglected "'way out in right field."

For those of you who are hesitant to coach or to referee at this time, for whatever reason, perhaps adult soccer will give you a better appreciation of what the game is about. No doubt there are many other parents who would benefit from a loosely-organized team activity, so round them up!*
Wear a safe pair of tennis shoes, comfortable shorts and a shirt bring a slightly underinflated, large leather or rubber ball (28 inches in circumference), choose up sides, and play a new sport! Forget about rules, at least for the time being. Allow

---

*Overexuberant players should immediately be reminded that soccer presents many options to players of all ages, and that each player should seek that competitive level which most suits his needs.

any kind of a reasonable throw-in, ignore the offsides, change your goalkeeper frequently, if you want one at all, and by all means forget about enlisting the services of a referee.

Physical well-being and safe recreation are the main by-products of such activity, and this outweighs rule considerations. Remember that a kickabout is no more structured than a dip in the ocean! Play co-ed soccer, team-Mother soccer, grandparents' soccer, soccer-in-the-rain, soccer-in-the-snow, or soccer-in-the-mud, but have fun playing the game which has captivated so many!

(Photo by Bill Bowyers)
"Come on in, Mom and Dad. The water's fine."

(Photo by Oto Maxmilian)

"I am far more concerned with striving for perfection than in attaining it."
... Albert Schweitzer

17

SOMEONE TO LOOK UP TO

In America, soccer has been hiding its light under a bushel, even with a very respectable third place in World Cup play in 1930. Now, more than forty years after a triumph over England and after years of continued frustration by those who love the game, America's first genuine soccer superstar is with us.

Kyle Rote, Jr. of the Dallas Tornado in the North American Soccer League brings a most unlikely background to the game. Taller and more muscular than most players in his profession, son of a famous football player in Texas, he never kicked a soccer ball until he was almost 18. Even then, in his dedication to sports, soccer was only to improve his strength and coordination for football.

Six years after that first move with the ball, he now represents the best and most admired in American soccer. An aggressive, accomplished "header" and a selfless player, Rote has been seen and imitated by young players all over the United States. In a game sometimes known for violence, he has never been known to violate referees, opponents, or the laws of good conduct and fair play. Even in the disappointment of defeat, he has time for autographs and for the youthful adulation that accompanies stardom. Clinics and conferences between games will find him working diligently with youngsters.

A divinity student whose ministry for the moment is on the field, Rote is the much-publicized winner of television's Superstars competition. His disciplined mental attitude toward soccer aided him in preparing for the tough grind of competition in the unfamiliar sports of swimming, golf, bicycling, bowling, and tennis. Almost embarrassed by the publicity of the superstar world, Rote immediately returned to the familiar world of soccer. Kyle Rote scores goals and creates others, and is highly valued by his league and by his club. His endorsement of his game, typical of the man, is a message to parents: "The big thing that sold me on soccer is to be able to see a youngster who has no athletic ability at all go out on a soccer field, run around for 90 minutes or 60 minutes, come off the field with sweat on his face and, even though he may not have touched the ball once, at least he will feel like he's really done something for the team. And he'll enjoy the physical exercise aspect of it. Plus, it's been good for him physically." (Soccer World, April 1974.)

FOR THOSE WHO
WANT TO KNOW MORE . . .

A variety of material is now becoming available for soccer enthusiasts.

BOOKS

Csanadi, Arpad, *Soccer*, Budapest, 1965. Very complete, and the best available source of training and coaching material. Available through the periodicals listed below.

Harris, Paul and Harris, Larry, *Fair or Foul?* The Complete Guide to Soccer Officiating in America. Available from Soccer For Americans, Box 836, Manhattan Beach, California 90266; 256 pages, written for soccer referees and coaches. Revised edition, 1975.

Vogelsinger, Hubert, *The Challenge of Soccer, A Handbook of Skills, Techniques, and Strategy.* Allyn and Bacon, Boston, 1973. Very helpful and complete on all aspects of the game.

Woosnam, Phil and Gardner, Paul, *Sports Illustrated Soccer.* J.B. Lippincott and Company, Philadelphia, 1972. A short paperback on skills by the Commissioner of the North American Soccer League. Young players will like it.

PERIODICALS

Soccer America, Box 9393, Berkeley, California. America's first national weekly, with scores, features, and special items of interest. Deals with all levels of the game in America.

Soccer Monthly, 4010 Empire State Building, New York, New York 10001. The official publication of the United States Soccer Federation. Many good features.

Soccer World, Box 366, Mountain View, California 94040. Well-researched articles and features appear bi-monthly.

FILM

"The Master and His Method" distributed by Alex Leslie, MGS Services, 619 W. 54th Street, New York, N.Y. 10019. Sponsored by Pepsi Cola, this series of 6 instructional films featuring Pele of Brazil is an excellent way to introduce soccer skills to both parents and players. Experienced players and coaches will learn from it as well.

ADDRESSES

Federation Internationale de Football Association (FIFA) Hitziweg 11, Zurich, Switzerland 8032
FIFA is the world governing body of soccer.

The United States Soccer Federation
4010 Empire State Building, New York, N.Y. 10001
The USSF is the national governing body for professional and amateur soccer in the United States.

SOME AFTERTHOUGHTS

To some people, soccer is existence itself, the struggle of people everywhere, life in microcosm. Even Shakespeare, in COMEDY OF ERRORS takes note of soccer:

> *"Am I so round with you as you with me*
> *That like a football you do spurn me thus?*
> *You spurn me hence and he will spurn me hither*
> *If I last in this service you must case me in leather."*
>
> Dromio of Ephesus, Act II

Soccer is akin to life. There are periods of rest, of an all-out effort, of medium performance, of joy and of tears. The span of a game allows for the ball in and out of play, when one re-evaluates and takes stock of individual and group performance.

Soccer may be what George Leonard had in mind when he wrote in The Intellectual Digest: "Sports are too beautiful and profound for simplistic slogans. How we play the game may turn out to be more important than we imagine, for it signifies nothing less than our way of being in the world."

True, the game may be studied and enjoyed on many levels. Pele the genius is viewed in the film previously mentioned with the following words as background: "Goals result from the brain as well as from the feet." This applies even in youth soccer.

The parent who wants to proceed to levels beyond this book will soon realize that soccer is deceptive in its simplicity. Out of the simplicity comes the beauty of a planned attack, placements rather than kicks, feints rather than "running over" an opponent, of the many moves where the ball becomes an extension of the player, and where goals are earned by probing and cleverness, not by mere kicking, and finally where it is understood that it is easier to frustrate an attack than it is to mount one.

And, whether you take up the position at the top of the stadium, where chess-like patterns emerge, or closer to the field of play, where the deft skills of individual and collective motion are present, you will find yourself "in" the game. More important for you and your child is not whether you participate, but rather what you experience from that participation.

DEFINITIONS AND TERMS

Advantage — A clause in the Laws of the Game which allows the Referee the freedom not to call fouls if a player or team is not disadvantaged by a foul.

Catenaccio — (You can impress your friends with this one). Any form of extreme or exaggerated defensive play.

Caution — An official disciplinary action taken by the Referee to a player who: (a) persistently infringes on the Laws of the Game (b) shows dissent by word or action from any decision given by the Referee (c) is guilty of ungentlemanly conduct and (d) enters or leaves the field without the permission of the Referee.

Center — A pass that moves the ball from the outside to the middle of the field.

Center Circle — The circle with the 10 yard radius at the center of the field.

Center Forward — (see Striker). The center player in the offensive attack, usually the tallest and strongest of the forwards.

Center Line — A straight line connecting the two touchlines at midfield, dividing the field into two equal halves.

Charging — The maneuver of using a shoulder against an opponent's to gain an advantage. This is legal.

Corner Area — The arc at each corner of the field from which corner kicks are taken. Also called corner circle, or quarter arc.

Corner Kick — A direct free kick from the corner area, taken by the attacking team when the defense last played a ball over the goal line.

Cross — A pass from one side of the field to the other, usually near the goal.

Dead Ball — A ball not in play. Also, a ball which is lying still, but playable.

Diagonal System — The universally accepted method of officiating, in which the Referee runs on a diagonal from one corner of the field to the other, aided by two Linesmen with flags.

Direct Free Kick — Any free kick which may be played directly into the goal without having to touch another player.

Dribbling — Controlling the ball by oneself, and moving it with the feet.

Drop Ball — A ball dropped by the Referee between two players after a temporary suspension in play. Contrary to all other methods of restarting play, neither team has an advantage as a result of a drop ball, unless it is dropped very near a goal.

Fair Charge — A charge is fair only with the shoulder, when the ball is within playing distance. Fair charging of the goalkeeper is not usually allowed in youth soccer. When it is, the goalkeeper must be in possession of the ball, and within the goal area.

Free Kick — An unchallenged kick, awarded by the Referee for an infringement.

Fullbacks — (Also called backs.) Those players who are the last line of defense, immediately in front of the goalkeeper. They should be strong and aggressive.

Goal Area — The area immediately in front of the goal, 20 by 6 yards in size.

Goalkeeper — The last line of defense, the player with the different-colored shirt who may touch the ball within the penalty area. He may go anywhere else on the field as well, and in doing so is treated as any other player.

Goal Kick — A kick taken from the goal area after the ball was last played by the attacking team over the goal line.

Goal Line — The line marking the end of the field, including that line under the crossbar.

Halfback — A midfield player who works between the defense and offense, and who has responsibilities for mounting attacks and repelling them.

Indirect Free Kick — A kick which must touch another player before a goal may be scored. The Referee will always raise his hand prior to the taking of indirect free kicks.

Insides — The two players positioned on either side of the center forward, normally called "inside right" and "inside left." They are relied upon for goals and for defensive help as well.

Intentional Foul — Intentional fouls are not always deliberate. In officiating a game, the Referee must judge the premeditation of the player. If a player willfully and repeatedly tries to gain an advantage by unfair means, then his acts are deliberate. However, if his violations are sporadic and generally non-disruptive to the continuance of the game without incident, his acts are to be judged intentional, and penalized, but not subject to disciplinary action.

Kickabout — An informal game of soccer, strictly for exercise.

Kick-Off — A place kick from the center of the field as a method of starting play after a goal has been scored or at the beginning of a period.

Linesmen — Under the diagonal system of game control, the officials who carry flags while running along the touchlines. They are responsible for calling offsides and balls in and out of play, and an occasional foul which the Referee cannot see.

Mark — As in "marking" a player. Staying close to an opponent, in order to keep him from obtaining the ball.

Linkmen — Halfbacks.

Obstruction — The attempt to "Play" the opponent and not the ball, by impeding his progress on the field. Penalized by an indirect free kick.

Offside — A player is offside when he is nearer to his opponent's goal line than the ball at the moment the ball was played, except in the five instances covered in Law XI.

Offside Position — A player is in an offside position when, technically, he could be called "offsides", but he is not taking advantage of his position.

Outsides — The two forwards on the two extreme outside of the attacking players. They operate near the touchlines, and are usually responsible for taking corner kicks and for placing the ball in the middle for the insides and the center forward. They should be the fastest players on the team, their speed enabling them to outrun fullbacks and to pick up long passes. (Also called Wings, or Wingers.)

Penalty Area — The 18x44 yard area immediately in front of the goal. The goalkeeper may handle the ball here.

Penalty Kick — If one of the nine penal offenses (see Law XII) is committed within the penalty area, a penalty kick results. No one other than the kicker may be closer than ten yards to the ball, and the goalkeeper must be on the goal line between the posts before the kick is taken.

Penalty Spot — A spot, twelve yards from the goal line, from which penalty kicks are taken.

Referee — The sole arbiter in a soccer game. The Referee usually works alone on the field, in concert with two Linesmen, who run on the touchlines. High school and college rules strongly recommend two referees on the field, international rules require only one, with Linesmen.

Speedball — A game which combines the skills and action of basketball and soccer. An excellent co-educational activity for developing familiarity with soccer.

Striker — The leader of the offensive attack, usually the center forward.

Sweeper — A roving, dependable defensive player whose assignment is to back up the play of other defensemen.

Tackle — The means of taking the ball from an opponent with one's feet. It may be made while standing or sliding.

Tennis Ball — Bet we surprised you with this one! There is no better way to develop ball control than by playing tennis without the racquet and with the feet.

Throw-in — When the ball goes across the touchline, it is put in play by the opponents of the team that touched it last. The ball must be completely across the line, on the ground or in the air, before it is considered out of play. The ball must be delivered from behind the head, with a part of each foot on the ground. The ball must enter the field from the point where it went out.

Touchlines — The side markings on the field, from which throw-ins are made.

Trapping — Stopping and containing the ball with some part of the body.

Volleying — Changing the direction of a ball with the foot, without allowing the ball to touch the ground. A half-volley will allow a short hop on the ball, as with a "drop kick."

Wall — A barrier of defenders positioned to aid the goalkeeper in defense against a free kick near the goal. The wall must be ten yards from the ball, or on the goal line between the goal posts.

Wall Pass — A pass from one player to another, using the second player as a wall. The ball is immediately returned to the passer, as a "give and go" in basketball. This is very effective when two players are confronted with only one opponent.

Wings — (Also called Wingers.) See Outsides.

(Photo by Gary Weaver)
It takes active people to keep an organization going.

FIFA LAWS OF THE GAME

LAW 1

(1) **Dimensions.** The field of play shall be rectangular, its length being not more than 130 yards nor less than 100 yards and its breadth not more than 100 yards nor less than 50 yards. (In International Matches the length shall be not more than 120 yards nor less than 110 yards and the breadth not more than 80 yards nor less than 70 yards.) The length shall in all cases exceed the breadth.

(2) **Marking.** The field of play shall be marked with distinctive lines, not more than 5 inches in width, not by a V-shaped rut, in accordance with the plan, the longer boundary lines being called the touch-lines and the shorter the goal-lines. A flag on a post not less than 5 ft. high and having a non-pointed top, shall be placed at each corner; a similar flag-post may be placed opposite the halfway line on each side of the field of play, not less than 1 yard outside the touch-line. A halfway-line shall be marked out across the field of play. The centre of the field of play shall be indicated by a suitable mark and a circle with a 10 yards radius shall be marked round it.

(3) **The Goal-Area.** At each end of the field of play two lines shall be drawn at right-angles to the goal-line, 6 yards from each goal-post. These shall extend into the field of play for a distance of 6 yards and shall be joined by a line drawn parallel with the goal-line. Each of the spaces enclosed by these lines and the goal-line shall be called a goal-area.

(1) **In** International matches the dimensions of the field of play shall be: maximum 110 x 75 metres; minimum 100 x 64 metres.
(2) National Associations must adhere strictly to these dimensions. Each National Association organising an International Match must advise the Visiting Association, before the match, of the place and the dimensions of the field of play.
(3) The Board has approved this table of measurements for the Laws of the Game:

		Metres
130 yards	. . . . .	120
120 yards	. . . . .	110
110 yards	. . . . .	100
100 yards	. . . . .	90
80 yards	. . . . .	75
70 yards	. . . . .	64
50 yards	. . . . .	45
18 yards	. . . . .	16.50
12 yards	. . . . .	11
10 yards	. . . . .	9.15
8 yards	. . . . .	7.32
6 yards	. . . . .	5.50
1 yard	. . . . .	1
8 feet	. . . . .	2.44
5 feet	. . . . .	1.50
28 inches	. . . . .	0.71
27 inches	. . . . .	0.68
5 inches	. . . . .	0.12
3/4 inch	. . . . .	0.019
1/2 inch	. . . . .	0.0127
3/8 inch	. . . . .	0.010

(4) The goal-line shall be marked the same width as the depth of the goal-posts and the cross-bar, so that the goal-line and goal-posts will conform to the same interior and exterior edges.

(4) **The Penalty-Area.** At each end of the field of play two lines shall be drawn at right-angles to the goal-line, 18 yards from each goal-post. These shall extend into the field of play for a distance of 18 yards and shall be joined by a line drawn parallel with the goal-line. Each of the spaces enclosed by these lines and the goal-line shall be called a penalty-area. A suitable mark shall be made within each penalty-area, 12 yards from the mid-point of the goal-line, measured along an undrawn line at right-angles thereto. These shall be the penalty-kick marks. From each penalty-kick mark an arc of a circle, having a radius of 10 yards, shall be drawn outside the penalty-area.

(5) **The Corner-Area.** From each corner-flag post a quarter circle, having a radius of 1 yard, shall be drawn inside the field of play.

(6) **The Goals.** The goals shall be placed on the centre of each goal-line and shall consist of two upright posts, equidistant from the corner-flags and 8 yards apart (inside measurement), joined by a horizontal cross-bar the lower edge of which shall be 8 ft. from the ground. The width and depth of the goal-posts and the width and depth of the cross-bars shall not exceed 5 inches (12 cm). The goal-posts and the cross-bars shall have the same width.

Nets may be attached to the posts, cross-bars and ground behind the goals. They should be appropriately supported and be so placed as to allow the goal-keeper ample room.

Footnote:

Goal nets. The use of nets made of hemp, jute or nylon is permitted. The nylon strings may, however, not be thinner than those made of hemp or jute.

(5) The 6 yards (for the outline of the goal-area) and the 18 yards (for the outline of the penalty-area) which have to be measured along the goal-line, must start from the inner sides of the goal-posts.

(6) The space within the inside areas of the field of play includes the width of the lines marking these areas.

(7) All Associations shall provide standard equipment, particularly in International Matches, when the Laws of the Game must be complied with in every respect and especially with regard to the size of the ball and other equipment which must conform to the regulations. All cases of failure to provide standard equipment must be reported to F.I.F.A.

(8) In a match played under the Rules of a Competition if the cross-bar becomes displaced or broken play shall be stopped and the match abandoned unless the cross-bar has been repaired and replaced in position or a new one provided without such being a danger to the players. A rope is not considered to be a satisfactory substitute for a cross-bar.

In a Friendly Match, by mutual consent, play may be resumed without the cross-bar provided it has been removed and no longer constitutes a danger to the players. In these circumstances, a rope may be used as a substitute for a cross-bar. If a rope is not used and the ball crosses the goal-line at a point which in the opinion of the Referee is below where the cross-bar should have been he shall award a goal.

The game shall be restarted by the Referee dropping the ball at the place where it was when play was stopped.

(9) National Associations may specify such maximum and minimum dimensions for the cross-bars and goal-posts, within the limits laid down in Law I, as they consider appropriate.

(10) Goal-posts and cross-bars must be made of wood, metal or other approved material as decided from time to time by the International F.A. Board. They may be

square, rectangular, round, half-round or elliptical in shape. Goal-posts and cross-bars made of other materials and in other shapes are not permitted.

(11) 'Curtain-raisers' to International matches should only be played following agreement on the day of the match, and taking into account the condition of the field of play, between representatives of the two Associations and the Referee (of the International Match).

(12) National Associations, particularly in International Matches, should restrict the number of photographers and have a line marked at least 2 metres and not more than 10 metres from the goal-lines and a similar distance from the angle formed by the goal-line with the touchlines; they should prohibit photographers from passing over these lines and finally forbid the use of artifical lighting in the form of 'flashlights'.

LAW II. – THE BALL

The ball shall be spherical; the outer casing shall be of leather or other approved materials. No material shall be used in its construction which might prove dangerous to the players.

The circumference of the ball shall not be more than 28 in. and not less than 27 in. The weight of the ball at the start of the game shall not be more than 16 oz. nor less than 14 oz. The pressure shall be equal to one atmosphere, which equals 15 lb./sq.in. (= 1 kg/cm^2) at sea level. The ball shall not be changed during the game unless authorised by the Referee.

(1) The ball used in any match shall be considered the property of the Association or Club on whose ground the match is played, and at the close of play it must be returned to the Referee.

(2) The International Board, from time to time, shall decide what constitutes approved materials. Any approved material shall be certified as such by the International Board.

(3) The Board has approved these equivalents of the weights specified in the Law: 14 to 16 ounces = 396 to 453 grammes.

(4) If the ball bursts or becomes deflated during the course of a match, the game shall be stopped and restarted by dropping the new ball at the place where the first ball became defective.

(5) If this happens during a stoppage of the game (place-kick, goal-kick, corner-kick, free-kick, penalty-kick or throw-in) the game shall be restarted accordingly.

LAW III. – NUMBER OF PLAYERS

(1) A match shall be played by two teams, each consisting of not more than eleven players, one of whom shall be the goalkeeper.

(2) Substitutes may be used in any match played under the rules of a competition, subject to the following conditions:

(a) that the authority of the international association(s) or national association(s) concerned, has been obtained,

(b) that, subject to the restriction contained in the following paragraph (c) the rules of a competition shall state how many, if any, substitutes may be used, and

(c) that a team shall not be permitted to use more that two substitutes in any match.

(3) Substitutes may be used in any other match, provided that the two teams concerned reach agreement on a maximum number, not exceeding five, and that the terms of such agreement are intimated to the Referee, before the match. If the Referee is not informed, or if the teams fail to reach agreement, no more than two substitutes shall be permitted.

(4) Any of the other players may change places with the goalkeeper, provided that the Referee is informed before the change is made, and provided also, that the change is made during a stoppage in the game.

(5) When a goalkeeper or any other player is to be replaced by a substitute, the following conditions shall be observed:

(a) the Referee shall be informed of the proposed substitution, before it is made,

(b) the substitute shall not enter the field of play until the player he is replacing has left, and then only after having received a signal from the Referee,

(c) he shall enter the field during a stoppage in the game, and at the half-way line.

Punishment:

(a) Play shall not be stopped for an infringement of paragraph 4. The players concerned shall be cautioned immediately the ball goes out of play.

(b) For any other infringement of this

(1) The minimum number of players in a team is left to the discretion of National Associations.

(2) The Board is of the opinion that a match should not be considered valid if there are fewer than seven players in either of the teams.

(3) A competition may require that the referee shall be informed, before the start of the match, of the names of not more than five players, from whom the substitutes (if any) must be chosen.

(4) A player who has been ordered off before play begins may only be replaced by one of the named substitutes. The kick-off must not be delayed to allow the substitute to join his team.

A player who has been ordered off after play has started may not be replaced.

A named substitute who has been ordered off, either before or after play has started, may not be replaced (this decision only relates to players who are ordered off under Law XII. It does not apply to players who have infringed Law IV.)

(5) A player who has been replaced shall not take any further part in the game.

(6) A substitute shall be deemed to be a player and shall be subject to the authority and jurisdiction of the Referee whether called upon to play or not. For any offence committed on the field of play a substitute shall be subject to the same punishment as any other player whether called upon or not.

law, the player concerned shall be cautioned, and if the game is stopped by the Referee, to administer the caution, it shall be re-started by an indirect free-kick, to be taken by a player of the opposing team, from the place where the ball was, when play was stopped.

LAW IV. – PLAYERS' EQUIPMENT

(1) A player shall not wear anything which is dangerous to another player.

(2) Footwear (boots or shoes) must conform to the following standard:

(a) Bars shall be made of leather or rubber and shall be transverse and flat, not less than half an inch in width and shall extend the total width of the sole and be rounded at the corners.

(b) Studs which are independently mounted on the sole and are replaceable shall be made of leather, rubber, aluminium, plastic or similar material and shall be solid. With the exception of that part of the stud forming the base, which shall not protrude from the sole more than one quarter of an inch, studs shall be round in plan and not less than half an inch in diameter. Where studs are tapered, the minimum diameter of any section of the stud must not be less than half an inch. Where metal seating for the screw type is used, this seating must be embedded in the sole of the footwear and any atachment screw shall be part of the stud. Other than the metal seating for the screw type of stud, no metal plates even though covered with leather or rubber shall be worn, neither studs which are threaded to allow them to be screwed on to a base screw that is fixed by nails or otherwise to the soles of footwear, nor studs which, apart from the base, have any form of protruding edge rim or relief marking or ornament, should be allowed.

(c) Studs which are moulded as an integral part of the sole and are not replaceable shall be made of rubber, plastic, polyurethene

(1) The usual equipment of a player is a jersey or shirt, shorts, stockings and footwear. In a match played under the rules of a competition, players need not wear boots or shoes, but shall wear jersey or shirt, shorts, or track suit or similar trousers, and stockings.

(2) The Law does not insist that boots or shoes must be worn. However, in competition matches Referees should not allow one or a few players to play without footwear when all the other players are so equipped.

(3) In International Matches, International Competitions, International Club Competitions and friendly matches between clubs of different National Associations, the Referee, prior to the start of the game, shall inspect players' boots and prevent any player whose boots do not conform to the requirements of Law IV from playing until they comply with the Law. Leagues and Competitions may include a similar provision in their rules.

(4) If the Referee finds that a player is wearing articles not permitted by the Laws and which may constitute a danger to other players, he shall order him to take them off. If he fails to carry out the Referee's instruction, the player shall not take part in the match.

(5) A player who has been prevented from taking part in the game or a player who has been sent off the field for infringing Law IV must report to the Referee during a stoppage of the game and may not enter or re-enter the field of play unless and until the Referee has satisfied himself that the player is no longer infringing Law IV.

or similar soft materials. Provided that there are no fewer than ten studs on the sole, they shall have a minimum diameter of three eights of an inch (10 mm.). In all other respects they shall conform to the general requirements of this Law.

(d) Combined bars and studs may be worn, provided the whole conforms to the general requirements of this Law. Neither bars nor studs on the soles shall project more than three-quarters of an inch. If nails are used they shall be driven in flush with the surface.

(3) The goalkeeper shall wear colours which distinguish him from the other players and from the referee.

Punishment: For any infringement of this Law, the player at fault shall be sent off the field of play to adjust his equipment and he shall not return without first reporting to the Referee, who shall satisfy himself that the player's equipment is in order; the player shall only re-enter the game at a moment when the ball has ceased to be in play.

LAW V. – REFEREES

A Referee shall be appointed to officiate in each game. His authority and the exercise of the powers granted to him by the Laws of the Game commence as soon as he enters the field of play.

His power of penalising shall extend to offences committed when play has been temporarily suspended, or when the ball is out of play. His decision on points of fact connected with the play shall be final, so far as the result of the game is concerned. He shall:

(a) Enforce the Laws.

(b) Refrain from penalising in cases where he is satisfied that, by doing so, he would be giving an advantage to the offending team.

(c) Keep a record of the game; act as timekeeper and allow the full or agreed

(6) A player who has been prevented from taking part in a game or who has been sent off because of an infringement of Law IV, and who enters or re-enters the field of play to join or re-join his team, in breach of the conditions of Law XII, shall be cautioned. If the Referee stops the game to administer the caution, the game shall be restarted by an indirect free-kick, taken by a player of the opposing side, from the place where the offending player was when the Referee stopped the game.

(1) Referees in International Matches shall wear a blazer or blouse the colour of which is distinct from the colours worn by the contesting teams.

(2) Referees for International Matches will be selected from a neutral country unless the countries concerned agree to appoint their own officials.

(3) The Referee must be chosen from the official list of International Referees. This need not apply to Amateur and Youth International Matches.

(4) The Referee shall report to the appropriate authority misconduct or any misdemeanour on the part of spectators, officials, players, named substitutes or other persons which take place either on the field of play or in its vicinity at any time prior to, during, or after the match in question so

time, adding thereto all time lost through accident or other cause.

(d) Have discretionary power to stop the game for any infringement of the Laws and to suspend or terminate the game whenever, by reason of the elements, interference by spectators, or other cause, he deems such stoppage necessary. In such a case he shall submit a detailed report to the competent authority, within the stipulated time, and in accordance with the provisions set up by the National Association under whose jurisdiction the match was played. Reports will be deemed to be made when received in the ordinary course of post.

(e) From the time he enters the field of play, caution any player guilty of misconduct or ungentlemanly behaviour and, if he persists, suspend him from further participation in the game. In such cases the Referee shall send the name of the offender to the competent authority, within the stipulated time, and in accordance with the provisions set up by the National Association under whose jurisdiction the match was played. Reports will be deemed to be made when received in the ordinary course of post.

(f) Allow no person other than the players and linesmen to enter the field of play without his permission.

(g) Stop the game if, in his opinion, a player has been seriously injured; have the player removed as soon as possible from the field of play, and immediately resume the game. If a player is slightly injured, the game shall not be stopped until the ball has ceased to be in play. A player who is able to go to the touch or goal-line for attention of any kind, shall not be treated on the field of play.

(h) Send off the field of play, any player who, in his opinion, is guilty of violent conduct, serious foul play, or the use of foul or abusive language.

(i) Signal for recommencement of the game after all stoppages.

that appropriate action can be taken by the Authority concerned.

(5) Linesmen are assistants of the Referee. In no case shall the Referee consider the intervention of a Linesman if he himself has seen the incident and from his position on the field, is better able to judge. With this reserve, and the Linesman neutral, the Referee can consider the intervention and if the information of the Linesman applies to that phase of the game immediately before the scoring or a goal, the Referee may act thereon and cancel the goal.

(6) The Referee, however, can only reverse his first decision so long as the game has not been restarted.

(7) If the Referee has decided to apply the advantage clause and to let the game proceed, he cannot revoke his decision if the presumed advantage has not been realised, even though he has not, by any gesture, indicated his decision. This does not exempt the offending player from being dealt with by the Referee.

(8) The Laws of the Game are intended to provide that games should be played with as little interference as possible, and in this view is the duty of Referees to penalise only deliberate breaches of the Law. Constant whistling for trifling and doubtful breaches produces bad feeling and loss of temper on the part of the players and spoils the pleasure of spectators.

(9) By para. (d) of Law V the Referee is empowered to terminate a match in the event of grave disorder, but he has no power or right to decide, in such event, that either team is disqualified and thereby the loser of the match. He must send a detailed report to the proper authority who alone has power to deal further with this matter.

(10) It a player commits two infringements of a different nature at the same time, the Referee shall punish the more serious offence.

(11) It is the duty of the Referee to act upon the information of neutral Linesmen

(j) Decide that the ball provided for a match meets with the requirements of Law II.

with regard to incidents that do not come under the personal notice of the Referee.

(12) The Referee shall not allow any person to enter the field until play has stopped, and only then, if he has given him a signal to do so, nor shall he allow coaching from the boundary lines.

LAW VI. – LINESMEN

Two Linesmen shall be appointed, whose duty (subject to the decision of the Referee) shall be to indicate when the ball is out of play and which side is entitled to the corner-kick, goal-kick or throw-in. They shall also assist the Referee to control the game in accordance with the Laws. In the event of undue interference or improper conduct by a Linesman, the Referee shall dispense with his services and arrange for a substitute to be appointed. (The matter shall be reported by the Referee to the competent authority.) The Linesmen should be equipped with flags by the Club on whose ground the match is played.

(1) Linesmen, where neutral, shall draw the Referee's attention to any breach of the Laws of the Game of which they become aware if they consider that the Referee may not have seen it, but the Referee shall always be the judge of the decision to be taken.

(2) National Associations are advised to appoint official Referees of neutral nationality to act as Linesmen in International Matches.

(3) In International Matches Linesmen's flags shall be of a vivid colour, bright reds and yellows. Such flags are recommended for use in all other matches.

(4) A Linesman may be subject to disciplinary action only upon a report of the Referee for unjustified interference or insufficient assistance.

LAW VII. – DURATION OF THE GAME

The duration of the game shall be two equal periods of 45 minutes, unless otherwise mutually agreed upon, subject to the following: (a) Allowance shall be made in either period for all time lost through accident or other cause, the amount of which shall be a matter for the discretion of the Referee; (b) Time shall be extended to permit a penalty-kick being taken at or after the expiration of the normal period in either half.

(1) If a match has been stopped by the Referee, before the completion of the time specified in the rules, for any reason stated in Law V it must be replayed in full unless the rules of the competition concerned provide for the result of the match at the time of such stoppage to stand.

(2) Players have a right to an interval at half-time.

At half-time the interval shall not exceed five minutes except by consent of the Referee.

LAW VIII. – THE START OF PLAY

(a) **At the beginning of the game,** choice of ends and the kick-off shall be decided by the toss of a coin. The team winning the toss shall have the option of choice of ends or the kick-off. The Referee having given a signal, the game shall be started by a player taking a place-kick (i.e., a kick at the ball while it is stationary on the ground in the centre of the field of play) into his opponents' half of the field of play. Every player shall be in his own half of the field and every player of the team opposing that of the kicker shall remain not less than 10 yards from the ball until it is kicked-off; it shall not be deemed in play until it has travelled the distance of its own circumference. The kicker shall not play the ball a second time until it has been touched or played by another player.

(b) **After a goal has scored,** the game shall be restarted in like manner by a player of the team losing the goal.

(c) **After half-time;** when restarting after half-time, ends shall be changed and the kick-off shall be taken by a player of the opposite team to that of the player who started the game.

Punishment. For any infringement of this Law, the kick-off shall be retaken, except in the case of the kicker playing the ball again before it has been touched or played by another player; for this offence, an indirect free-kick shall be taken by a player of the opposing team from the place where the infringement occurred. A goal shall not be scored direct from a kick-off.

(d) **After any other temporary suspension;** when restarting the game after a temporary suspension of play from any cause not mentioned elsewhere in these Laws, provided that immediately prior to the suspension the ball has not passed over the touch or goal-

(1) If, when the Referee drops the ball, a player infringes any of the Laws before the ball has touched the ground, the player concerned shall be cautioned or sent off the field according to the seriousness of the offence, but a free-kick cannot be awarded to the opposing team because the ball was not in play at the time of the offence. The ball shall therefore be again dropped by the Referee.

(2) Kicking-off by persons other than the players competing in a match is prohibited.

lines, the Referee shall drop the ball at the place where it was when play was suspended and it shall be deemed in play when it has touched the ground; if, however, it goes over the touch or goal-lines after it has been dropped by the Referee, but before it is touched by a player, the Referee shall again drop it. A player shall not play the ball until it has touched the ground. If this section of the Law is not complied with the Referee shall again drop the ball.

LAW IX. – BALL IN AND OUT OF PLAY

The ball is out of play:

(a) When it has wholly crossed the goal-line or touch-line, whether on the ground or in the air.

(b) When the game has been stopped by the Referee.

The ball is in play at all other times from the start of the match to the finish including:

(a) If it rebounds from a goal-post, cross-bar or corner-flag post into the field of play.

(b) If it rebounds off either the Referee or Linesmen when they are in the field of play.

(c) In the event of a supposed infringement of the Laws, until a decision is given.

(1) The lines belong to the areas of which they are the boundaries. In consequence, the touch-lines and the goal-lines belong to the field of play.

LAW X. – METHOD OF SCORING

Except as otherwise provided by these Laws, a goal is scored when the whole of the ball has passed over the goal-line, between the goal-posts and under the cross-bar, provided it has not been thrown, carried or propelled by hand or arm, by a player of the attacking side, except in the case of a goal-keeper, who is within his own penalty-area.

(1) Law X defines the only method according to which a match is won or drawn; no variation whatsoever can be authorised.

(2) A goal cannot in any case be allowed if the ball has been prevented by some outside agent from passing over the goal-line. If this happens in the normal course of play, other than at the taking of a penalty-kick: the game must be stopped and restarted by the

The team scoring the greater number of goals during a game shall be the winner; if no goals, or an equal number of goals are scored, the game shall be termed a "draw".

Referee dropping the ball at the place where the ball came into contact with the interference.

(3) If, when the ball is going into goal, a spectator enters the field before it passes wholly over the goal-line, and tries to prevent a score, a goal shall be allowed if the ball goes into goal unless the spectator has made contact with the ball or has interfered with play, in which case the Referee shall stop the game and restart it by dropping the ball at the place where the contact or interference occurred.

LAW XI. – OFF-SIDE

A player is off-side if he is nearer his opponents' goal-line than the ball **at the moment the ball is played unless:**

(a) He is in his own half of the field of play.

(b) There are two of his opponents nearer to their own goal-line than he is.

(c) The ball last touched an opponent or was last played by him.

(d) He receives the ball direct from a goal-kick, a corner-kick, a throw-in, or when it was dropped by the Referee.

Punishment. For an infringement of this Law, an indirect free-kick shall be taken by a player of the opposing team from the place where the infringement occurred.

A player in an off-side position shall not be penalised unless, in the opinion of the Referee, he is interfering with the play or with an opponent, or is seeking to gain an advantage by being in an offside position.

(1) Off-side shall not be judged at the moment the player in question receives the ball, but at the moment when the ball is passed to him by one of his own side. A player who is not in an off-side position when one of his colleagues passes the ball to him or takes a free-kick, does not therefore become offside if he goes forward during the flight of the ball.

LAW XII. – FOULS AND MISCONDUCT

A player who intentionally commits any of the following nine offences:

(a) Kicks or attempts to kick an opponent;
(b) Trips an opponent, i.e., throwing or attempting to throw him by the use of the legs or by stooping in front of or behind him;
(c) Jumps at an opponent;
(d) Charges an opponent in a violent or dangerous manner;
(e) Charges an opponent from behind unless the latter be obstructing;
(f) Strikes or attempts to strike an opponent;
(g) Holds an opponent with his hand or any part of his arm;
(h) Pushes an opponent with his hand or any part of his arm;
(i) Handles the ball, i.e., carries, strikes or propels the ball with his hand or arm. (This does not apply to the goalkeeper within his own penalty-area);

shall be penalised by the award of a **direct free-kick** to be taken by the opposing side from the place where the offence occurred.

Should a player of the defending side intentionally commit one of the above nine offences within the penalty-area he shall be penalised by a **penalty-kick.**

A penalty-kick can be awarded irrespective of the position of the ball, if in play, at the time an offence within the penalty-area is committed.

A player committing any of the five following offences:

1. Playing in a manner considered by the Referee to be dangerous, e.g., attempting to kick the ball while held by the goalkeeper;
2. Charging fairly, i.e., with the shoulder, when the ball is not within playing distance of the players concerned and they are definitely not trying to play it;
3. When not playing the ball, intentionally obstructing an opponent, i.e., running

(1) If the goalkeeper either intentionally strikes an opponent by throwing the ball vigorously at him or pushes him with the ball while holding it, the Referee shall award a penalty-kick, if the offence took place within the penalty-area.

(2) If a player deliberately turns his back to an opponent when he is about to be tackled, he may be charged but not in a dangerous manner.

(3) In case of body-contact in the goal-area between an attacking player and the opposing goalkeeper not in possession of the ball, the Referee, as sole judge of intention, shall stop the game if, in his opinion, the action of the attacking player was intentional, and award an indirect free-kick.

(4) If a player leans on the shoulders of another player of his own team in front of him in order to head the ball, which he succeeds in doing, the Referee shall stop the game, caution the player for ungentlemanly conduct and award an indirect free-kick to the opposing side.

(5) A player's obligation when joining or rejoining his team after the start of the match to 'report to the Referee' must be interpreted as meaning 'to draw the attention of the Referee from the touch-line'. The signal from the Referee shall be made by a definite gesture which makes the player understand the he may come into the field of play; it is not necessary for the Referee to wait until the game is stopped, (this does not apply in respect of an infringement of Law IV) but the Referee is the sole judge of the moment in which he gives his signal of acknowledgement.

(6) The letter and spirit of Law XII do not oblige the Referee to stop a game to administer a caution. He may, if he chooses, apply the advantage. If he does apply the advantage, he shall caution the player when play stops.

(7) If a player covers up the ball without touching it in an endeavour not to have it played by an opponent, he obstructs but

between the opponent and the ball, or interposing the body so as to form an obstacle to an opponent;
4. Charging the goalkeeper except when he
   (a) is holding the ball;
   (b) is obstructing an opponent;
   (c) has passed outside his goal-area;
5. When playing as goalkeeper,
   (a) takes more than 4 steps whilst holding, bouncing or throwing the ball in the air and catching it again without releasing it so that it is played by another player, or
   (b) indulges in tactics which, in the opinion of the Referee, are designed merely to hold up the game and thus waste time and so give an unfair advantage to his own team

shall be penalised by the award of an **indirect free-kick** to be taken by the opposing side from the place where the infringement occurred.

A player shall be **cautioned** if:

(j) he enters or re-enters the field of play to join or rejoin his team after the game has commenced, or leaves the field of play during the progress of the game (except through accident) without, in either case, first having received a signal from the Referee showing him that he may do so. If the Referee stops the game to administer the caution the game shall be restarted by an indirect free-kick taken by a player of the opposing team from the place where the offending player was when the referee stopped the game. If, however, the offending player has committed a more serious offence he shall be penalised according to that section of the law he infringed;

(k) he persistently infringes the Laws of the Game;

(l) he shows by word or action, dissent from any decision given by the Referee;

(m) he is guilty of ungentlemanly conduct.

For any of these last three offences, in addition to the caution, an **indirect free-kick**

does not infringe Law XII para. 3 because he is already in possession of the ball and covers it for tactical reasons whilst the ball remains within playing distance. In fact, he is actually playing the ball and does not commit an infringement; in this case, the player may be charged because he is in fact playing the ball.

(8) If a player intentionally stretches his arms to obstruct an opponent and steps from one side to the other, moving his arms up and down to delay his opponent, forcing him to change course, but does not make "bodily contact" the Referee shall caution the player for ungentlemanly conduct and award an indirect free-kick.

This applies also to players who attempt to prevent the goalkeeper from putting the ball into play in accordance with Law XII, 5 (a).

(9) If after a Referee has awarded a free-kick a player protests violently by using abusive or foul language and is sent off the field, the free-kick should not be taken until the player has left the field.

(10) Any player, whether he is within or outside the field of play, whose conduct is ungentlemanly or violent, whether or not it is directed towards an opponent, a colleague, the Referee, a linesma, or other person, or who uses foul or abusive language, is guilty of an offence, and shall be dealt with according to the nature of the offence committed.

(11) If, in the opinion of the Referee a goalkeeper intentionally lies on the ball longer than is necessary, he shall be penalised for ungentlemanly conduct and
(a) be cautioned and an indirect free-kick awarded to the opposing team;
(b) in case of repetition of the offence, be sent off the field.

(12) The offence of spitting at opponents, officials or other persons, or similar unseemly behaviour shall be considered as violent conduct within the meaning of section (n) of Law XII.

shall also be awarded to the opposing side from the place where the offence occurred unless a more serious infringement of the Laws of the Game was committed.

A player shall be **sent off** the field of play, if:

(n) in the opinion of the Referee he is guilty of violent conduct or serious foul play;

(o) he uses foul or abusive language

(p) he persists in misconduct after having received a caution.

If play be stopped by reason of a player being ordered from the field for an offence without a separate breach of the Law having been committed, the game shall be resumed by an **indirect free-kick** awarded to the opposing side from the place where the infringement occurred.

(13) If, when a Referee is about to caution a player, and before he has done so, the player commits another offence which merits a caution, the player shall be sent off the field of play.

LAW XIII. – FREE-KICK

Free-kicks shall be classified under two headings: "Direct" (from which a goal can be scored direct against the offending side), and "Indirect" (from which a goal cannot be scored unless the ball has been played or touched by a player other than the kicker before passing through the goal).

When a player is taking a direct or an indirect free-kick inside his own penalty-area, all of the opposing players shall remain outside the area, and shall be at least ten yards from the ball whilst the kick is being taken. The ball shall be in play immediately it has travelled the distance of its own circumference and is beyond the penalty-area. The goalkeeper shall not receive the ball into his hands, in order that he may thereafter kick it into play. If the ball is not kicked direct into play, beyond the penalty-area, the kick shall be retaken.

When a player is taking a direct or an indirect free-kick outside his own penalty-area, all of the opposing players shall be at least ten yards from the ball, until it is in

(1) In order to distinguish between a direct and an indirect free-kick, the Referee, when he awards an indirect free-kick, shall indicate accordingly by raising an arm above his head. He shall keep his arm in that position until the kick has been taken.

(2) Players who do not retire to the proper distance when a free-kick is taken must be cautioned and on any repetition be ordered off. It is particularly requested of Referees that attempts to delay the taking of a free-kick by encroaching should be treated as serious misconduct.

(3) If, when a free-kick is being taken, any of the players dance about or gesticulate in a way calculated to distract their opponents, it shall be deemed ungentlemanly conduct for which the offender(s) shall be cautioned.

play, unless they are standing on their own goal-line, between the goal-posts. The ball shall be in play when it has travelled the distance of its own circumference.

If a player of the opposing side encroaches into the penalty-area, or within ten yards of the ball, as the case may be, before a free-kick is taken, the Referee shall delay the taking of the kick, until the Law is complied with.

The ball must be stationary when a free-kick is taken, and the kicker shall not play the ball a second time, until it has been touched or played by another player.

Punishment. If the kicker, after taking the free-kick, plays the ball a second time before it has been touched or played by another player an indirect free-kick shall be taken by a player of the opposing team from the spot where the infringement occurred.

LAW XIV. – PENALTY-KICK

A penalty-kick shall be taken from the penalty-mark and, when it is being taken, all players with the exception of the player taking the kick, and the opposing goalkeeper, shall be within the field of play but outside the penalty-area, and at least 10 yards from the penalty-mark. The opposing goalkeeper must stand (without moving his feet) on his own goal-line, between the goal-posts, until the ball is kicked. The player taking the kick must kick the ball forward; he shall not play the ball a second time until it has been touched or played by another player. The ball shall be deemed in play directly it is kicked, i.e., when it has travelled the distance of its circumference, and a goal may be scored direct from such a penalty-kick. If the ball touches the goalkeeper before passing between the posts, when a penalty-kick is being taken at or after the expiration of half-time or full-time, it does

(1) When the Referee has awarded a penalty-kick, he shall not signal for it to be taken, until the players have taken up position in accordance with the Law.

(2) (a) If, after the kick has been taken, the ball is stopped in its course towards goal, by an outside agent, the kick shall be retaken.

(b) If, after the kick has been taken, the ball rebounds into play, from the goalkeeper, the cross-bar or a goal-post, and is then stopped in its course by an outside agent, the Referee shall stop play and restart it by dropping the ball at the place where it came into contact with the outside agent.

(3) (a) If, after having given the signal for a penalty-kick to be taken, the Referee sees that the goalkeeper is not in his right place on the goal-line, he shall, nevertheless, allow the kick to proceed. It shall be retaken, if a goal is not scored.

(b) If, after the Referee has given the signal for a penalty-kick to be taken, and

not nullify a goal. If necessary, time of play shall be extended at half-time or full-time to allow a penalty-kick to be taken.

Punishment:

For any infringement of this Law:

(a) by the defending team, the kick shall be retaken if a goal has not resulted.

(b) by the attacking team other than by the player taking the kick, if a goal is scored it shall be disallowed and the kick retaken.

(c) by the player taking the penalty-kick, committed after the ball is in play, a player of the opposing team shall take an indirect free-kick from the spot where the infringement occurred.

before the ball has been kicked, the goalkeeper moves his feet, the Referee shall, nevertheless, allow the kick to proceed. It shall be retaken, if a goal is not scored.

(c) If, after the Referee has given the signal for a penalty-kick to be taken, and before the ball is in play, a player of the defending team encroaches into the penalty-area, or within ten yards of the penalty-mark, the Referee shall, nevertheless, allow the kick to proceed. It shall be retaken, if a goal is not scored.

The player concerned shall be cautioned.

(4) (a) If, when a penalty-kick is being taken, the player taking the kick is guilty of ungentlemanly conduct, the kick, if already taken, shall be retaken, if a goal is scored.

The player concerned shall be cautioned.

(b) If, after the referee has given the signal for a penalty-kick to be taken, and before the ball is in play, a colleague of the player taking the kick encroaches into the penalty-area or within ten yards of the penalty-mark, the Referee shall, nevertheless, allow the kick to proceed. If a goal is scored, it shall be disallowed, and the kick retaken.

The player concerned shall be cautioned.

(c) If, in the circumstances described in the foregoing paragraph, the ball rebounds into play from the goalkeeper, the cross-bar or a goal-post, the Referee in addition to cautioning the player, shall stop the game, and award an indirect free-kick to the opposing team, to be taken from the place where the infringement occurred.

(5) (a) If, after the referee has given the signal for a penalty-kick to be taken, and before the ball is in play, the goalkeeper moves from his position on the goal-line, or moves his feet, and a colleague of the kicker encroaches into the penalty-area or within 10 yards of the penalty-mark, the kick, if taken, shall be retaken.

The colleague of the kicker shall be cautioned.

(b) If, after the Referee has given the signal for a penalty-kick to be taken, and before the ball is in play, a player of each team encroaches into the penalty-area, or within 10 yards of the penalty-mark, the kick, if taken, shall be retaken.

The players concerned shall be cautioned.

(6) When a match is extended, at half-time or full-time, to allow a penalty-kick to be taken or retaken, the extension shall last until the moment that the penalty-kick has been completed, i.e. until the Referee has decided whether or not a goal is scored.

A goal is scored when the ball passes wholly over the goal-line.

(a) direct from the penalty-kick,

(b) having rebounded from either goal-post or the cross-bar, or

(c) having touched or been played by the goalkeeper.

The game shall terminate immediately the Referee has made his decision.

(7) When a penalty-kick is being taken in extended time:

(a) the provisions of all of the foregoing paragraphs, except paragraphs (2) (b) and (4) (c) shall apply in the usual way, and

(b) in the circumstances described in paragraphs (2) (b) and (4) (c) the game shall terminate immediately the ball rebounds from the goalkeeper, the cross-bar or the goal-post.

LAW XV. – THROW-IN

When the whole of the ball passes over a touch-line, either on the ground or in the air, it shall be thrown in from the point where it crossed the line, in any direction, by a player of the team opposite to that of the player who last touched it. The thrower at the moment of delivering the ball must face the field of play and part of each foot shall be either on the touch-line or on the ground outside the touch-line. The thrower shall use both hands and shall deliver the ball from behind and over his head. The ball

(1) If a player taking a throw-in, plays the ball a second time by handling it within the field of play before it has been touched or played by another player, the Referee shall award a direct free-kick.

(2) A player taking a throw-in must face the field of play with some part of his body.

(3) If, when a throw-in is being taken, any of the opposing players dance about or gesticulate in a way calculated to distract or impede the thrower, it shall be deemed ungentlemanly conduct, for which the offender(s) shall be cautioned.

shall be in play immediately it enters the field of play, but the thrower shall not again play the ball until it has been touched or played by another player. A goal shall not be scored direct from a throw-in.

Punishment:

(a) If the ball is improperly thrown in the throw-in shall be taken by a player of the opposing team.

(b) If the thrower plays the ball a second time before it has been touched or played by another player, an indirect free-kick shall be taken by a player of the opposing team from the place where the infringement occurred.

LAW XVI. – GOAL-KICK

When the whole of the ball passes over the goal-line excluding that portion between the goal-posts, either in the air or on the ground, having last been played by one of the attacking team, it shall be kicked direct into play beyond the penalty-area from a point within that half of the goal-area nearest to where it crossed the line, by a player of the defending team. A goalkeeper shall not receive the ball into his hands from a goal-kick in order that he may thereafter kick it into play. If the ball is not kicked beyond the penalty-area, i.e., direct into play, the kick shall be retaken. The kicker shall not play the ball a second time until it has touched – or been played by – another player. A goal shall not be scored direct from such a kick. Players of the team opposing that of the player taking the goal-kick shall remain outside the penalty-area whilst the kick is being taken.

Punishment: If a player taking a goal-kick plays the ball a second time after it has passed beyond the penalty-area, but before it has touched or been played by another player, an indirect free-kick shall be awarded to the opposing team, to be taken from the place where the infringement occurred.

(1) When a goal-kick has been taken and the player who has kicked the ball touches it again before it has left the penalty-area, the kick has not been taken in accordance with the Law and must be retaken.

LAW XVII. – CORNER-KICK

When the whole of the ball passes over the goal-line, excluding that portion between the goal-posts, either in the air or on the ground, having last been played by one of the defending team, a member of the attacking team shall take a corner-kick, i.e., the whole of the ball shall be placed within the quarter circle at the nearest corner-flag-post, which must not be moved, and it shall be kicked from that position. A goal may be scored direct from such a kick. Players of the team opposing that of the player taking the corner-kick shall not approach within 10 yards of the ball until it is in play, i.e., it has travelled the distance of its own circumference, nor shall the kicker play the ball a second time until it has been touched or played by another player.

Punishment:

(a) If the player who takes the kick plays the ball a second time before it has been touched or played by another player, the Referee shall award an indirect free-kick to the opposing team, to be taken from the place where the infringement occurred.

(b) For any other infringement the kick shall be retaken.

PELE: THE MASTER

(Photos by Oto Maxmilian)

Edson Arantes do Nascimento (Pele) of Brazil now plays soccer in the United States, for the New York Cosmos. When he first came to America, more than ten years ago, large crowds came to see his magic.

They crowded around him before the game.

And as the game progressed . . .

Desperation moves were tried to keep the ball away from him . . .

Sometimes he ended up on the ground, but bounced right up . . .

To show his perfect form . . .

And when it was all over, he was still smiling, as the opposition finally
trapped him in an elevator, without his shoes.